T0194928

FASTING GOD'S WAY

Reverend Clayton Driggs

WESTBOW
PRESS®
A DIVISION OF THOMAS NELSON
& ZONDERVAN

WestBow Press books may be ordered through booksellers or by contacting:

WestBow Press
A Division of Thomas Nelson & Zondervan
1663 Liberty Drive
Bloomington, IN 47403
www.westbowpress.com
1 (866) 928-1240

ISBN: 978-1-9736-1002-1 (sc)
ISBN: 978-1-9736-1004-5 (hc)
ISBN: 978-1-9736-1003-8 (e)

Library of Congress Control Number: 2017918059

Print information available on the last page.

WestBow Press rev. date: 01/02/2018

My Vision

To see the keys of the kingdom of heaven in the hand of every believer, promoting unity and teamwork in Christ Jesus until the kingdom of heaven is clearly manifested on earth so the world know that God sent Jesus Christ from heaven to earth

This book is dedicated to the Holy Spirit. He has been my closest companion in life and was the true author of the revelations that are in this book. In spite of who I have been or what I did, He has never withheld God's goodness from me.

I am extremely grateful for the transformation God the Holy Spirit has made within me.

I must also express gratitude to my wife, Roumona McDavid-Driggs, for her great patience with me. She's been my greatest supporter in this venture. She nurtured the seed of this book by her encouraging words. The time spent writing this book was a great sacrifice on her part, but she never complained about it; instead, she supported me all the way.

I love you, sweetie pea.

In your relationships with one another, have the same mindset as Christ Jesus: Who, being in very nature God, did not consider equality with God something to be used to His own advantage; rather, He made himself nothing by taking the very nature of a servant, being made in human likeness. And being found in appearance as a man, He humbled himself by becoming obedient to death even death on a cross!

—Philippians 2:4–8

CONTENTS

FOREWORD

About the time this book was being published, a deranged young man walked into a small country church and began randomly shooting the worshipers. When he finished his rampage, more than two dozen innocent souls were killed. It is an evil day and the world has become a very dangerous place to exist. It is no coincidence that we are on earth in a time such as this, for God has chosen for us to live in these times. You see, I believe our witness of hope and love will make a difference for those we know and meet. In fact, God has promised power to overcome all the powers of the enemy. Yet, we must accept that evil will not be overcome with human strategies or by the feeble attempts of believers who fail to realize this battle as a spiritual one. Our battles are not with flesh and blood but against principalities and spirits loosed upon the earth for a season to tempt, deceive and destroy. But don't be afraid, we are not defenseless against the evil of this world. We have been given power.

My friend, Reverend Clayton Driggs has written a powerful tool on the subject of fasting. It is for believers who wish to live in the victory God has provided. In it you will find the guidance of a man who walks with God and who has been empowered to invest in each of us with the power of his words. As an act of obedience, he has penned this tremendous work on this very relevant topic. I trust him and I trust his desire to invest what God has invested in him to every person who picks up this book.

Fasting is not easy. Jesus once fasted for forty days in the desert and during that physically weakened time the devil sought to tempt Jesus to forgo His divine purpose in exchange for human satisfaction. The devil is still doing that to believers today through subtle and suggestive means. But the devil can be overcome by the Word of God and seasons of prayer and fasting. There is a call of God to fast and one should be sensitive to the timing of God for seasons of prolonged fasting.

It has always been my conviction that in fasting, my spiritual sensitivities are heightened and God speaks. You too will find God in your fasting. Though God is not hiding, I think He lingers on the periphery to understand your hunger for Him, for relationship with Him, for your decision to forsake all, risk all in pursuit of His presence and His power in your life. As you read this book, it is my prayer that you will find the Savior in powerful and life-changing ways. He is ready to be found by you and it may be that He will reveal Himself to you as you encounter Clayton's heart in the writing. There is power in the words of this book. I'm glad Clayton wrote them and I'm glad you hold a copy of my friend's outstanding work.

These words seem appropriate from the Lord through the prophet Jeremiah, who wrote: "For I know the thoughts that I think toward you, says the Lord, thoughts of peace and not of evil, to give you a future and a hope. Then you will call upon Me and go and pray to Me, and I will listen to you. And you will seek Me and find *Me*, when you search for Me with all your heart. (Jeremiah 29:11-13, NKJV)

Dr. William E. (Bill) Isaacs
Executive Director
Center for Pastoral Excellence
Lagrange, Ohio
2017

FOREWORD

Many believers have long since recognised the importance of prayer and fasting in the life of a Christian. What many struggle with however is understand the place of fasting and how do we go about effectively engaging in it.

Do we not all know of individuals and churches who at least once a year (often at the beginning of the New Year) engages in times of fasting and prayer. For many, these times of fasting have become nothing more than a tradition or the fulfilling of a routine. Fasting and prayer is indeed much more than an annual exercise. The scripture is clear on the topic and spoke to the issue much more than you may have recognised. God has not left us in the dark on this important subject of prayer and fasting.

It is said that "a man with an experience is never at the mercy of a man with knowledge". On reading this book it very apparent that Reverend Driggs wrote this book out of the bowels of experience. His knowledge and perspectives on the issue is refreshing and provides an abundance of insights to stir and challenge the learned and mature believer as well as the young believer just embarking on this journey of faith.

One will find his views on legitimate and illegitimate fasting to be quite sound and particularly insightful

As a person who has engaged in many individual and collective times of fasting and prayer, this book provided me with not just valuable insights but some practical tools that Pastors, leaders, and individuals, would also find helpful in making their times of prayer and fast much more meaningful.

It is my prayer and sincere hope that persons reading this book would come to experience the joy and fulfilment that comes to one who engages in a time of prayer and fast.

I congratulate Reverend Driggs on the writing of a great book indeed a powerful resource to the Body of Christ.

Bishop Don Douglas
Education Director
New Testament Church of God
Trinidad & Tobago

PREFACE

I still can vividly remember when the Lord started to teach me about fasting in the way that truly pleases Him. It was in the year 2012, when the church that I pastored was about to begin the Daniel's fast. We'd done this fast every year since I'd become the pastor, but that year something different happened. A few days before the fast began, I received the church mail, and with it was a book on fasting. The book was called *Fasting That Moves God's Hands* by T. L. Lowery. Initially, I thought of leaving the book with all the other books that we kept at the church. But then I thought, *If I don't read, I won't learn*. I heard the Spirit speak within me: "My people enter into captivity for a lack of knowledge." He was prompting me to read and learn, so I took the book home and read a portion of it every morning during my devotions. During that time, my eyes were opened to the power of fasting. All the examples of God's hand at work when people fasted caught my heart. I wanted to be one of them. That year's fast was intentional and full of clarity. I thank God that He chose to teach me by way of that book. From that year on, I was better motivated to fast because I had a much better understanding of fasting and its wonderful outcomes.

The following year—but later in the year—I came across a book called *Fasting* by Jentezen Franklin. I was extremely motivated and enlightened by the testimonies in that book. The Lord used *Fasting* to introduce me to my first forty-day fast. Immediately after reading those books, I found and listened to YouTube videos of Christian teachers who taught about fasting. I thank God greatly for T. L. Lowery and Jentezen Franklin, for their books were the sparks that ignited a fire within me and fanned the flame to cause me to have a fasting life.

With regard to this book, I must give all the credit to the Holy Spirit. The Lord "downloaded" the contents of this book into my spirit and mind. It all started as sermons on the topic of fasting during my forty-day fast, and the Lord kept opening my understanding of the scriptures about fasting. For six Sundays I preached on fasting, and each sermon was turned into a chapter in this book. I pray that the Lord will do for you what He did for me—ignite a fire in you that results in having a fasting life. As the apostle Paul prayed, "I pray that your eyes of understanding would be enlightened and that you would come into the knowledge of truth that transforms you." (Ephesians 1: 18). I desire that you will not just hear what I am saying but will see it. As Bishop David Oyedepo of Living World Church Worldwide said in one of his messages, "What you see you naturally believe, and what you believe you supernaturally become."

ACKNOWLEDGMENTS

I want to thank everyone who spoke over my life and told me that I would write books. First, thanks to Joe Daniel, an old junior secondary school friend from Trinidad, who was the first person to tell me I would write books; and to Ayesha William, who spoke a prophecy over my life about writing; and to Dr. Kevin White, who confirmed God's Word spoken over my life concerning my writing for the Lord. Mostly I would like to acknowledge my parents, Mr. Huan Driggs and Mrs. Patricia Castellano-Driggs, for investing in me so that I could be at this place of confidence to take up the call to write.

My deepest gratitude goes to Dr. Richard Yorke, who was a tremendous help to me. I could not have made it this far without his time and effort in editing this book. Also, thanks go to my brother-in-law Bishop Don Douglas (pastor of Irie Village New Testament Church of God, Trinidad and Tobago). After he enthusiastically read through the first draft of this book, he gave me some very constructive criticism. I was greatly motivated by his enthusiasm and comments.

Finally, my thanks to everyone who is a part of Love Without Walls and believes in the vision God has over my life. They were always concerned about my progress, with the expectation of great things to come. Thank you for praying for me and for the impact of this book in the lives of others. Thank you, and may God bless you all richly.

INTRODUCTION

There was a boy who was possessed with a demonic spirit that caused the boy to suffer from epilepsy. The evil spirit continually attempted to destroy the boy's destiny by making him have seizures and making him fall into the water or into the fire. Observing his son's situation, the concerned father knew that his son was not suffering with a mere illness but that a cruel spirit possessed the boy. Fortunately, the father had heard of Jesus and His disciples and how they went from town to town, healing sick people and casting out demons. The father found Jesus's disciples and asked them to make the demon leave his son.

Some time before, Jesus gave His disciples authority to cast demons out of people. The disciples saw so much success in doing so that they celebrated this newly given status. But this time it was different, for the demon would not leave the boy, despite the disciples' attempts to cast it out. This demon must have been very stubborn to resist the authority given to the disciples. I can only imagine what this stubborn demon did to the disciples' faith as it consistently refused to yield to the disciples' commands. A crowd gathered to see what was happening, and their peering eyes caused added pressure to the disciples' mission. But then Jesus showed up on the scene, and all attention was diverted toward Him.

The father of the demon-possessed boy approached Jesus and explained the situation to Him. He had lost faith in the disciples' ability to help his son, but he thought maybe Jesus could help. After explaining the boy's situation, the father then said to Jesus, "If you can do something, please help my son." Was it unreasonable for the father to make his request in such a manner? After all, he had just witnessed the close students of Jesus fail at the task. *Maybe this case is special. Maybe it is too hard for the disciples. What if it is too difficult for Jesus?* These questions may have plagued his mind, so his best approach to Jesus was a speculative attempt, a last resort. But Jesus immediately knew what to do, and the father's recital of the fiasco and his doubtful approach did not faze Jesus. He made an adjustment to the man's faith, and then, without breaking a sweat, He cast the demon out of the boy. The demon dared not resist Jesus and left at the word of His command.

If you are familiar with this story, you know that Jesus explained to the disciples why they could not cast the demon out of the boy. Once they began to doubt, it was downhill from that point. Yet Jesus revealed a key that the disciples did not have that would have helped them to cast out the demon. Jesus said, "However, this kind does not come out except by prayer and fasting." In saying this, Jesus informed His disciples that there are some spirits that do not listen to the commands of those who have been given authority and that another force is necessary. This force is a result of prayer and fasting. In Isaiah 58, fasting is described as a power to break chains, undo heavy burdens, set the captive free, and to break the yoke. This speaks not of authority but power. In other words, the one who lays down his or her life in fasting receives dynamic power to break the powers of bondage.

This is the answer to stubborn demons that seize and keep people in bondage. Because they do not respond to authority of the saints, it will take power to drive out such rebellious, stubborn demons. This is what fasting does for believers; it causes them to receive the yoke-breaking, chain-breaking power of God that will force any demon out and liberate the captive to walk in his or her God-given destiny.

As you read this book, I pray that God the Father will open your eyes to see the power of His love, which overcomes all evil, satanic, demonic powers of the world. May His love birth in you a passion to see freedom prevail, and through love you will fast to see this freedom come to people. The world is encountering many more stubborn, stiff-necked spirits—evil spirits of pleasures, addiction, and confusion and incurable diseases of all sorts. There are even filthy spirits of religion that creep into the church to make it powerless against the whims of Satan and principalities. These forces, though powerful and mighty against man, pale in comparison with the power of God's love. And there is no greater love that we can give than to lay down our lives in fasting for someone's freedom.

CHAPTER 1

Fasting: a Demonstration of Love

Fasting is picking up your cross, carrying it,
and dying on it for the sake of others;
only love drives one to do so.

In Isaiah 58, God used the prophet to tell us the dos and don'ts of fasting. In that chapter we can find God's expressed urgency to correct His people, showing them their shortcomings and revealing the erroneous perceptions His people had about fasting. This chapter reveals God's zeal to teach them the truth about fasting. Isaiah 58 shows us what God accepts as fasting, or what I'd like to call "fasting God's way." I will show you what the Lord showed me about true fasting.

Fasting! Fasting! Read All about It!

"Shout it aloud, do not hold back. Raise your voice like a trumpet. Declare to my people their rebellion and to the descendants of Jacob their sins" (Isaiah 58:1).

God told Isaiah to voice aloud the message about fasting and not to hold back from speaking plainly, so that everyone could hear and know what fasting truly was about. This shows that fasting was an important subject that God did not want His people to misunderstand. God used Isaiah to expose erroneous concepts and common failures people encounter when they fast in ignorance. Misunderstanding of what fasting is about will result in doing it the wrong way and, unfortunately, for the wrong reasons. It can be very frustrating when we make such a painful physical sacrifice, and it turns out to be a waste of time. For this reason, out of concern for us, God wants us to know the truth about what successful fasting entails. The Lord told Isaiah to make this information about fasting as public as possible so that Israel could know the truth about this important matter. I believe the Lord also wants me to be as loud as possible about fasting, and He prompted me to write this book. Although this book may not be audibly loud, I hope it seems to you that I am shouting from the mountains.

Don't Fool Yourself Because You're Not Fooling God

> "For day after day they seek me out; they seem eager to know my ways, as if they were a nation that does what is right and has not forsaken the commands of its God. They ask me for just decisions and seem eager for God to come near them. 'Why have we fasted,' they say, 'and you have not seen it? Why have we humbled ourselves, and you have not noticed?' "Yet on the day of your fasting, you do as you please and exploit all your workers. Your fasting ends in quarreling and strife, and in striking each other with wicked fists. You cannot fast as you do today and expect your voice to be heard on high." (Isaiah 58:2–4)

The verses above speak of a people who fasted while being deluded about what fasting was really about. God sent the prophet Isaiah to show them their faults in the way they fasted so that they could see where they went wrong and turn to what was right. The prophet exposed their misconceptions about fasting and, in essence, told them that their hearts were not saying what they thought their fasting was. By the act of fasting, Israel appeared to pursue God, but the motives for their fast showed that they were not truly pursuing Him. They were once again pursuing God's hand and not His ways.

God described them this way: "They seem eager to know my ways, as if they were a nation that does what is right and has not forsaken the commands of its God" (Isaiah 58:2). God wanted His people to know that forsaking His commands while they attempted to seek His response through fasting would only result in His silence. Fasting while neglecting God's commands meant that they were ignoring the most important part of fasting, which is love.

When the Pharisees asked Jesus what the greatest commandment was, Jesus recited what God told Moses in Deuteronomy 8. He said the greatest commandments were "to love God with their all, and to love their neighbor as they would love themselves." These are the commands Isaiah was referring to when he said, "They seem eager to know my ways, as if they were a nation that … has not forsaken the commands of God." Because Israel's fast was missing the key ingredient of love, God did not respond to their fast. This led to their frustration whenever they fasted and did not see results.

Fasting without love is a hypocritical trap from the deceiver. Do you know how Jesus addressed hypocrisy? He exposed it and those who practice it. This is another reason why God wanted Isaiah to cry aloud, to expose hypocritical traps concerning fasting so that everyone would hear and avoid them. Unfortunately, though the Bible contains scriptures that expose hypocritical traps about fasting, many individuals and churches today are still ensnared by them. But just as God told Isaiah to show His people their mistakes, I also appeal that if you fast without love, you are holding to the same fallacy Israel had in Isaiah's day. The problem with fallacies is in thinking you are right when the truth is that you are falling short of God's expectations. This is why it's so important to expose deceptive concepts about fasting so that everyone will know the truth, turn, and see God's healing power in and through their lives.

Fasting Starts in the Heart

The prophet Isaiah exposed purposes for fasting that we rarely consider as reasons for why people fast. Yet if we are not careful, we can be deluded through ignorance about fasting and have the same reasons for fasting of which the prophet spoke. Isaiah stated, "Behold, ye fast for strife and debate, and to smite with the fist of wickedness: ye shall not fast as ye do this day, to make your voice to be heard on high" (Isaiah 58:4 KJV).

When we take a closer look at strife and debate, we will find at its roots the selfish desire to win without consideration for others. Strife can be defined as "vigorous or bitter conflict," and debate refers to formal arguments. Both speak about disunity, segregation, separation, and an unwillingness to pay the price for a peaceful solution. Segregation and disunity are not what God desires of us. For this reason, God sent His Son Jesus Christ to restore the relationship between God and humankind and to promote peace among humans. So fasting for selfish reasons, with a desire to be blessed without consideration of others, is from a spirit of segregation and disunity. Think about it, Pastor, in your heart. Have you ever desired to have as many or more members than the church down the street? Have you approached God with that same heart in fasting, without any consideration for the more important matter—the souls? Brother and sister, have you desired a promotion for financial gain without concern for those you seek to be promoted over; yet you approached God in fasting without cleansing your heart of such a wicked perception? This kind of fasting will not be answered by God. These are a couple of examples of fasting for strife, debate, and to strike others with the fist of wickedness. For God called us not to seek our own interests but the interests of others. This is the way of love, and God is love.

What God was saying through Isaiah was that He evaluates our fast by its purpose and not by the act alone. We may think that intentionally refraining from eating tells God we are seeking Him, but God determines what we truly say by our purpose. Where some go wrong while fasting is in thinking they would never knowingly fast for the wrong reasons. But as I just stated, God does not look at fasting as the act alone. He first searches our hearts to see the true purpose for the fast, to determine if the fast is to be accepted. This should not come as a surprise to us, seeing that the truth concerning who we are and what we do is hidden in the heart.

In order to know the truth about another person, one must see that person's heart. God told Samuel, "Do not consider his appearance or his height, for I have rejected him. The LORD does not look at the things people look at. People look at the outward appearance, but the LORD looks at the heart" (1 Samuel 16:7). So God searches out hearts first to see the purpose for our fasting, to determine if we are eligible or ineligible to be heard by God when we fast. If our hearts are fixed on our own gain and self-preservation in fasting, then the purpose for our fast is a selfish one. If we do this, then the Lord can see that we have turned an act of love and selflessness into a deluded attempt to trick Him into blessing us. But fasting without the right motive results in silence from God, as He said, "You cannot fast as you do today and expect your voice to be heard on high" (Isaiah 58:4).

Prior to 2012, I used to see fasting as merely a time to pray for the things I wanted God to do for me while I abstained from eating food. Previously I would fast for things like finances, a job, a house, and such things. Someone may say, "How could it be wrong to fast for those things?" But as I stated previously, it all depends on the heart or the purpose behind the fast. If at the heart of all those desires is a selfish purpose to have and to increase or to be greater than others, then those desires are corrupted. Anyone who is fasting for selfish reasons is already saying that he or she is not thinking of anyone else but himself or herself. Whenever our hearts are self-centered, and the purpose for our fast is not for God's glory or for the blessing of the lives of others, then that fast is wrong. Even fasting for more of God's power can be a good thing that is tainted if it is done with the wrong motive. The question we should always ask ourselves before we fast is, "What is my true purpose for fasting?" Or "Who am I really concerned about that I have decided to fast?" If the answers are to see God gain glory through our lives in some way or to allow God to use us as a means of blessing someone else through this fast, then we should fast on, for God will hear us.

I've fasted many times and honestly thought that the heart of fasting was about abstaining from eating so that my inner man would become more sensitive to God. This is true regarding the mechanics of fasting, but in thinking this way, I confused the method with the purpose. The heart of fasting does not originate in the methods but in the purpose for fasting. Before 2012, I focused on the mechanics of fasting but was ignorant of the true purposes for fasting that would result in answers from God. When God opened my understanding to the true purposes for fasting, it revealed that my previous reasons for fasting included a lot of self-centered motives. In the past, I sought after my own gain in the fast. In my ignorance, I was motivated by selfish purposes for fasting, but God is not interested in self-centered deeds. The unspoken reason and hidden purposes are the things

God sees in our fast, and if it only involves us and our request before God, or our own growth, or even our own justice, then our fast is not pleasing unto God.

Just as selfishness is at the center of strife and quarreling, fasting without love or self-centered fasting results in strife and debate. Self-centered fasting can be compared to the fig tree that Jesus cursed because it only bore leaves and had no fruit. The presence of leaves without the fruit was uncommon for that type of fig tree because that it was known for bearing fruit while the leaves also were growing. The leaves were an indicator that the fruit ought to be present. But a life full of the "the indicator of righteousness" and no true fruit of righteousness is an indication of self-righteousness. Fruits are for others and not for the tree that bears it; leaves are for the tree to indicate to others that the fruit is present. If we look righteous but are not bearing the fruit of righteousness, then we have selfish motives for appearing righteous without being willing to show the proof of righteousness, which is love. And just as the fig tree was cursed because it only bore leaves, in the same way fasting for selfish reasons is cursed because it is unfruitful. But fasting with love in your heart results in fruits that bless others at your expense. Fasting without love only appears to be fruitful, but it is not beneficial to anyone, not even yourself. The fast that God requires is about others and not only about you!

Fasting is Making Yourself the Sacrifice

The first sacrifices that were offered unto God were those of Cain and Abel. The scripture records that God rejected Cain and his offering, for which Cain became angry. Notice how the scripture states it: "The LORD looked with favor on Abel and his offering, but on Cain and his offering he did not look with favor" (Genesis 4:4–5). Regarding sacrifices and offerings, God either accepts or rejects the person and his or her sacrifice but not just the sacrifice. God does this because the sacrifice finds its value in the heart of the one who sacrifices. One definition of *sacrifice*, according to Merriam-Webster dictionary, is "the destruction or surrender of something for the sake of something else." This definition describes the act of fasting. Fasting involves the destruction of the body for the sake of something or someone else by abstaining from necessary food. When we fast, we intentionally surrender our bodies as living sacrifices unto God. But the act alone, though it sounds noble in itself, is not enough to please God. And just as Cain and his sacrifice were rejected, so too we can be rejected, even though we present our own bodies as the sacrifice. What we must learn from God's rejection of Cain is that God will not reject the sacrifice of those who do it the right way, and the mere act of sacrificing does not warrant His approval.

The right way to offer the sacrifice of fasting unto God is to have a heart of love for God and others while we present the sacrifice to Him. This is required of every sacrifice that God calls us to make. We know that Cain and his offering were rejected because of what was in his heart as he offered his sacrifice. The scripture speaks about it in this way: "In the course of time Cain brought some of the fruits of the soil as an offering to the LORD. And Abel also bought an offering—fat portions from some of the firstborn of his flock. The Lord looked with favor on Abel and his offering, but on Cain and his offering He did not look with favor. So Cain was very angry, and his face was downcast. Then the LORD said to Cain, "Why are you angry? Why is your face downcast?" (Genesis 4:3–6).

At first glance, the emphasis of this passage may appear to be on the type of sacrifices that were offered to God. I believe the type of sacrifice offered is of extreme importance, as this has a direct connection with the heart of the one who sacrifices. But when we look at the first thing God said in response to Cain, we see that He focused on Cain's attitude before speaking of his works, which related to the type of sacrifice he offered. God immediately addressed the issue that led to His disapproval of Cain's offering and spoke about the hidden matters of the heart.

I don't mean to say that the sacrifice itself does not matter to God, for it does. We must abstain from offering sacrifices that are illegitimate, unacceptable, and undesirable to God. But God determines the legitimacy of the sacrifice by the state of the heart that offers it. So the anger that Cain showed when Abel's sacrifice was accepted and his was rejected exposed the hate that was hiding in his heart, which made his sacrifice unacceptable to God in the first place. Later on in the story, God confronts Cain about the hate in his heart, but Cain does not address the issue. As time went on, in a moment when Cain was having a conversation with Abel, this unaddressed hatred in his heart led him to murder his own brother. It was this unaddressed hatred in his heart that caused God to reject Cain's sacrifice; it caused unwarranted anger and upset and eventually turned him into a murderer. If we are not careful, we could be fasting with a heart that makes our sacrifice like Cain's.

Jesus spoke about this heart issue when he said,

> "You have heard that it was said to the people long ago, 'You shall not murder, and anyone who murders will be subject to judgment.' But I tell you that anyone who is angry with a brother or sister will be subject to judgment. Again, anyone who says to a brother or sister, 'Raca,' is answerable to the court. And anyone who says, 'You fool!' will be in danger of the fire of hell. "Therefore, if you are offering your gift at the altar and there remember that your brother or sister has something against you, leave your gift there in front of the altar. First go and be reconciled to them; then come and offer your gift. "Settle matters quickly with your adversary who is taking you to court. Do it while you are still together on the way, or your adversary may hand you over to the judge, and the judge may hand you over to the officer, and you may be thrown into prison. Truly I tell you, you will not get out until you have paid the last penny." (Matthew 5:21–26)

We see from what Jesus said that our offerings or sacrifices are polluted when we have the wrong heart toward others while we offer our sacrifices. Jesus counsels us to get our hearts right through repentance and reconciliation before offering sacrifices unto God. He tells us to do this so that we and our sacrifices will not be rejected. Hate is not the only pollutant that defiles the sacrifice of fasting, but anything that makes the act of sacrificing about yourself and not God and others pollutes your fast. This is why it is so important to know how to fast the right way, having the right heart. Anyone who offers himself or herself to God as a sacrifice in fasting and says "Lord, me" is saying, "I lay down my life for my own gain." Instead, when we fast we ought to say, "Lord, use me."

Isaiah described the fast God chooses like this: "Is not this the kind of fasting I have chosen: to loose the chains of injustice and untie the cords of the yoke, to set the oppressed free and break every yoke? Is it not to share your food with the hungry and to provide the poor wanderer with shelter—when you see the naked, to clothe them, and not to turn away from your own flesh and blood?" (Isaiah 58:6–7). If we rephrase verses 6 and 7, we would see a definition for fasting that goes like this: "Fasting God's way involves becoming a sacrifice for others. It is the laying down of your life for the sake of others, represented by the refusal to meet your own physical needs so that as a sacrifice, you can be used to meet the needs of others."

One of the conditions of a sacrifice unto God is that it replaces or stands in the gap for another; that is, one life for another. This is true love, and so for the sacrifice of fasting to be true before God, it must possess the ingredient *love*, or it is not true fasting. Simply put, God expects a sacrifice that is good, and a good sacrifice is a pure person who gives up his or her own life, food, or any other thing that person needs to preserve his or her life on behalf of another. This is the sacrifice God hears and blesses.

Fasting Is Seeking to Be Blessed So You Can Be a Blessing

There is a prayer recorded in the book of John in which Jesus prays to the Father in this way: "After Jesus said this, he looked toward heaven and prayed: "Father, the hour has come. Glorify your Son, that your Son may glorify you" (John 17:1). In what way was Jesus seeking to be glorified? I believe the glory Jesus asked for in this prayer was the glory of the seed. The glory of the seed is its ability to come to life after it is buried in the ground. After a seed is buried, in due season it rises from its burial place, as though it has come back to life. Then it is transformed into the image of a fruit-bearing tree, ready to produce fruit for the glory of the one who planted the seed. In other words, "Give me glory so I can give You glory." Another way to say this is, "Bless me so that I may bless You." When we fast and ask God to bless us, our reason should be so that we can become a fruitful blessing to God after we lay down our bodies in fasting.

Another scripture speaks of the Lord's telling Abram to give up his father's covering and customs to go to a place God would show him. Then God said, "I will make you into a great nation, and I will bless you; I will make your name great, and you will be a blessing" (Genesis 12:2). Here again we see that God first blesses us so that we can be a blessing. But what was first required for Abram to be blessed? To give up his covering and customs and go to a place God wanted him to go. So Abram was asked to give up what once sustained him to become a vessel through which God could bless others. For God told him, "I will bless those who bless you, and whoever curses you I will curse; and all peoples on earth will be blessed through you" (Genesis 12:3). This must be our reason for our sacrifice in fasting, to give up what sustains us so that God can pour out blessings into our lives, through which we bless others.

Love Must Be the Origin of Our Fasts

As I began to write on these topics, the Holy Spirit dropped this rhyme in my spirit:

> Purposes are found at the beginning of all things,
> and at the beginning of true fasting one will find God's plan.
> Results are found at the end of all things,
> and at the end of true fasting one will find God's hand.
> So if you desire to see God's healing hand,
> to see Him do what no one else can,
> then begin where His face can be found,
> in His loving plan.

As I pondered on this rhyme, I realized that God wants us to be participants in what He is doing, He wants to share the experience with us. But if we try to get involved in what He is doing without first knowing the plan, then we only make a mess of things. This is what we do when we fast while looking for results but never take the time to know God's purpose for our fasting. To be a useful part of the work that God is doing, we must put our faces where He first puts His; that is, in His plans. When we encounter Him in the planning stage, then we can be exceedingly effective for Him in the *doing* stages.

When I was in Trinidad and Tobago, the Lord told me, "As soon as you get there, fast for seven days." This was after I had learned about the power of love in our fasts. During that time I prayed for the souls of people in the nation, people I did not know personally. After ending the fast, by orchestration of the Holy Ghost, my wife and mother-in-law had a brilliant idea to go to Mayaro to my wife's aunt's house and spend a few days there. Unknown to us, God was preparing to answer the request I'd made in the fast for people I did not know. We got to Mayaro on Tuesday night, and on Wednesday night I was invited to attend a crusade. While I was there, I was asked to preach the following night. I went there with great anticipation. I knew that all was prepared for the people to receive the gift of God. A love offering was given prior to the crusade in fasting. And though I did not know them, God's love for them was manifested in my fast. After I preached the good news of Jesus Christ and His power to restore destines, I addressed the people who were listening from their homes and were not under the tent where we were. As I told them how they could receive Jesus Christ into their hearts, I noticed movement in front of me. Two young men walked from my left side to my right, but I kept on speaking. When I turned my attention to the people under the tent to invite them come to Jesus, my wife tapped me on the shoulder to draw my attention to what was happening behind me. As I turned around, I saw a crowd of about twenty-five to thirty people standing there, waiting to accept Jesus in their hearts and for prayer. Without a call or a plea for them to come, the Holy Spirit had drawn them to Jesus Christ. I witnessed the power of love that night. Love is a great power from God that is at the foundation of everything He does. If we understand the power of love, we also can see the power of love that engages God to draw all men unto Him. As Jesus said, "And I, when I am lifted up from the earth, will draw all people to myself" (John 12:32). Jesus expressed the love of God on the earth by dying on a cross, and by this act of love we were drawn to Him. If we express the same act of love by fasting in Christ's name for others, we too will see people drawn unto Jesus Christ.

Previously I mentioned that fasting is becoming a sacrifice; it is seeking to be blessed so that you can be a blessing to others. The purpose of becoming a sacrifice is to express God's love to others through your life. God's purpose for sacrifices always has been to make a payment for the needs of another in love, so fasting is a payment made to the Lord on behalf of others in love. Fasting is one of the many ways we are to lay down our lives for our friends in obedience to the command of our Lord. In the book of John, Jesus spoke about love in this manner: "Greater love has no one than this: to lay down one's life for one's friends" (John 15:13). This scripture describes love at its best, when someone sacrifices his or her life for others. This means the sacrifice of fasting is one of the ultimate expressions of love.

Jesus also said this about love: "If you keep my commands, you will remain in my love, just as I have kept my Father's commands and remain in his love" (John 15:10). When Jesus said, "If you keep my commands," it was the same as saying, "If My words remain in you …" But look at the significance of having His words effectively dwelling in us, as it is stated again in the book of John: "If you remain in me and my words remain in you, ask whatever you wish, and it will be done for you" (John 15:7). You see, it is the keeping of God's commandment of love, and the hiding of His Word in our hearts that makes us eligible to ask what we will and to have the guarantee that it will be done.

Whenever we exclude love for other from our fasting, we break Jesus's command, and position ourselves to be rejected. This is what Isaiah warned the people about when he said, "For day after day they seek me out; they seem eager to know my ways, as if they were a nation that does what is right and has not forsaken the commands of its God" (Isaiah 58:2). But as Isaiah again stated, "You cannot fast as you do today and expect your voice to be heard on high" (Isaiah 58:4).

Jesus gave us this commandment: "My command is this: Love each other as I have loved you" (John 15:12). This is the commandment that the people of Isaiah's day forsook, as some do today. And how did Jesus love us? He loved us by laying down His life for our sake. So you see, love warrants God's response to our prayer when we fast. Love from God within us calls unto the loving God in heaven, just as "deep calls to deep" (Psalms 42:7).

CHAPTER 2

Avoid Illegitimate Fasting

The scripture records the lives of King Saul and King David and shows us the contrast in the way they respected and trusted God and His commands and the way they honored God's prophets and cared for His people. I will use these two kings to show you examples of fasting that did and did not please God. One of these two kings made illegitimate fasts, and the other fasted God's way.

In 1 Samuel 24, the scripture records an event where Saul and Israel's army were in hot pursuit of the Philistines. And Saul, in his zeal, told the army to fast until the end of the day—he thought that fasting would cause him to defeat his enemies. Let me set the backdrop. Saul recently had become the king of Israel and was zealous in showing the people what he would do as their king. He fought against the Philistines and sought to destroy them completely. One day when the Philistine army was warring against Israel, Jonathan, the king's son, and his armor-bearer fought against the Philistine army. The Lord began to give Israel victory over the Philistines through Jonathan and his armor-bearer alone. So when the Israelite army joined them, they won a great victory that day. But as Israel was pursuing the Philistines, Saul, in his zeal, made the people take an oath that no one would eat anything until Saul had avenged his enemy. But when Saul made the people take the oath, Jonathan was not there to know about it.

Let's take a closer look at what happened, as it relates to fasting. I'll refer to the errors of Saul's and the army's fast as *illegitimate fasting*. In this event with King Saul, we can find the things that make a fast illegitimate in God's eyes.

Illegitimate Fasting Results in Confusion, Not Clarity

"Now the men of Israel were pressed to exhaustion that day, because Saul had placed them under an oath, saying, "Let a curse fall on anyone who eats before evening—before I have full revenge on my enemies." So no one ate anything all day" (1 Samuel 14:24).

Saul was seeking to impress the nation by destroying the entire Philistine army, and he thought that God would help him if he and his army fasted. Saul proclaimed a fast in the form of a command, an oath, and a curse, and being their king, the army was forced into it. Without any consideration for the army's well-being, he made them swear that they would fast until they accomplished the task. According to the word of the Lord to Isaiah, this fast was illegitimate, for God said, "Behold, in the day of your fast you seek your own pleasure, and oppress all your workers. Behold, you fast only to quarrel and to fight and to hit with a wicked fist. Fasting like yours this day will not make your voice to be heard on high" (Isaiah 58:3–5).

It was not irrational for Saul and the army to fast until they saw victory that day, for this kind of fasting was not uncommon. Daniel is one example; he purposed that he would not eat any "precious food," meaning pleasurable food for twenty-one days, until he got an answer from God. But the major difference between Saul and Daniel is that Daniel was laying his stomach on the line for the sake of the nation, but Saul was making the nation suffer for a personal aspiration. Saul even forced this fast on the army by adding a curse to it, declaring that a curse would fall on anyone who ate before evening. The driving force behind the fast, then, was their not wanting to be cursed; this also makes the fast illegitimate.

You may be thinking, *No one ever held a gun to my head to make me fast.* But have you ever fasted because you didn't want the other church members or the pastor to think that you were not committed to the church? Have you ever fasted because you did not want people to think that you didn't possess the self-discipline or the willingness to sacrifice for the greater good. Sadly, these are intimidating motivators that people submit to as hidden reasons for their fasts. What is even sadder is that those who fast for those reasons waste their time, because God does not hear those who fast because of motivations like those mentioned earlier. In other words, it would have been good *not* to fast if the reasons mentioned were the motivators for fasting. It would have been even better to quickly turn from self-centered purposes and genuinely seek the interest of God and others.

God does not hear the voices of those who fast for selfish reasons. Though the Israelite army fasted, things ended in confusion and not with God's favor. The story tells us that when that evening came, the people were so hungry they broke God's commands about eating meat with blood still in it. Then, to make things worse, Saul almost killed his own son at the end of the day. You see, Saul wanted to pursue the army but didn't consult God, and when he was reminded to pray, he did, but God did not answer him. Saul assumed that it was because someone broke the vow. They cast lots to see who had broken the oath, and the lot fell on Jonathan because he unknowingly ate honey during the fast. Now remember, Saul said, "Let a curse fall on anyone who eats before evening," and he was willing to kill his own son to honor the oath. But God did not allow the curse of death to stand, and He used the people to save Jonathan. Wow, to think that all this confusion happened at the end of a fast. But this is an example of the confusion we can experience when fasting in ways of which God does not approve.

When we fast illegitimately, we can be left confused, wondering why we did not get an answer from God. We may even assume that other apparently unholy people or things caused the answer not to come, and we don't realize that we are not heard if we fast illegitimately. So I'd like to encourage pastors and leaders not to call a fast hastily or ritually and not to force a fast upon people in the name of piety or even because of a so-called "church growth" agenda that brings you glory more than God. These and similar motives inevitably will lead to illegitimate fasting, which God does not receive. Instead of getting clarity about matters, there is confusion. Remember, whenever God is silent to our fasts, it's because the fasts are illegitimate.

Illegitimate Fasting Prevents Us from Receiving God's Sweet Word

"The entire army entered the woods, and there was honey on the ground. When they went into the woods, they saw the honey oozing out; yet no one put his hand to his mouth, because they feared the oath. But Jonathan had not heard that his father had bound the people with the oath, so he reached out the end of the staff that was in his hand and dipped it into the honeycomb. He raised his hand to his mouth, and his eyes brightened" (1 Samuel 14:25–27).

Just as David saw a cause to act when Goliath threatened the Israelite army, Jonathan saw a cause to fight the Philistine army, even though it was only him and his armor-bearer. Jonathan was not guided by a zealousness to please or impress others. Instead, like David his friend, he was willing to lay his life on the line for the sake of the army by the direction of the Lord. The scriptures say this of Jonathan: "Jonathan said to his young armor-bearer, "Come, let's go over to the outpost of those uncircumcised men. Perhaps the Lord will act in our behalf. Nothing can hinder the Lord from saving, whether by many or by few." (1 Samuel 14: 6). Later on we see that because he sacrificed his life for others, he was the only one who partook of what God prepared for the Israelite army. Instead of using fasting as a religious work in an attempt to sway God, Jonathan trusted God to reveal His plan. Like David, Jonathan was willing to offer his own life as a sacrifice in order for God to carry out His will; this is what fasting God's way is at its core.

When Jonathan and the army came to the time and place prepared for refreshment, Jonathan alone ate honey and was extraordinarily refreshed. This did not happen to Saul and his men. They were frustrated because of that silly fast. Please don't misunderstand me; I am not saying that fasting is silly or that not fasting is better than fasting. I am saying that to live according to God's plan, with the intent of pleasing God and caring for others, is better than assuming that the mere sacrifice of fasting would move God's hand. Remember, Saul learned this lesson the hard way.

The scriptures states, "But Samuel replied: "Does the Lord delight in burnt offerings and sacrifices as much as in obeying the Lord? To obey is better than sacrifice, and to heed is better than the fat of rams. For rebellion is like the sin of divination, and arrogance like the evil of idolatry. Because you have rejected the word of the Lord, he has rejected you as king" (1 Samuel 15:22–23). It was because of Saul's misconception of the purpose of sacrifices that he went astray from the will of God. But Jonathan understood that his life would bring glory to God if he yielded himself to be used by God on behalf of the people; this qualified him to receive the wisdom of God, and it placed him in God's will.

Being in the will of God, Jonathan made this wise statement: "My father has made trouble for us all!" Jonathan exclaimed. "A command like that only hurts us. See how refreshed I am now that I have eaten this little bit of honey. If the men had been allowed to eat freely from the food they found among our enemies, think how many more Philistines we could have killed!" (1 Samuel 14:29–30). The people saw Jonathan eat honey after his father, Saul, made the people take an oath not to eat. So they confronted Jonathan about it, and Jonathan's response inadvertently revealed the plan of God for Israel, but they were not able to partake of it. This was the wisdom of God I spoke about previously that Jonathan received; the wisdom that prompted him to reveal the true purpose for the honey. You see, God wanted to refresh the people with honey so that the mission could be more successful, but the illegitimate fast was in the way.

When we decide to take on a fast for our own ambition, we place ourselves in a position where we can't receive what God prepared for guaranteed success. One of the things that God prepares for us when we fast His way is a sweet word of wisdom. We see in the event with Saul, Jonathan, and the Israelite army that honey was waiting in the midst of the trees, sitting on the ground for easy access. God used the honey to teach us something very powerful about fasting. The scripture refers to honey in the psalms in this way: "The fear of the Lord is pure, enduring forever. The decrees of the Lord are firm, and all of them are righteous. They are more precious than gold, than much pure gold; they are sweeter than honey, than honey from the honeycomb" (Psalm 19:9–10).

The scripture also describes honey as gracious or helpful words. The book of Proverbs states: "Gracious words are a honeycomb, sweet to the soul and healing to the bones" (Proverb 16:24). When we put these two passages together, we see that the honey from the honeycomb that falls to the ground for easy access is the gracious words of God that are decreed upon those who fear the Lord. God used this event to show that illegitimate fasting prevents us from receiving a decree from the Lord, even the gracious word prepared for us by God. But if we are willing to fast in a manner where we make our lives the object of sacrifice, through which God can defeat the enemy in the lives of others, then we become eligible to receive the decrees of the Lord, the gracious helpful words that bring victory and strength for endurance.

The King James Version of the Bible says that when Jonathan tasted the honey "his eyes were enlightened." I really like the wording the King James Version uses because it lets us know that God desires to give us what enlightens us. God desires to give us understanding in the matters we're pursuing, but these moments of revelation and understanding were missed for many during their fasts. This was simply because they were fasting for the wrong reason, and their attention was in the wrong place.

I want you to know that the things I am telling you are true and will be a great blessing if you apply them to your life. The scripture states, "If any of you lacks wisdom, you should ask God, who gives generously to all without finding fault, and it will be given to you" (James 1:5).

When we ask God for wisdom, He promises to give it to us without reprimanding us. But if wisdom is withheld from us, especially during a fast, it means we are out of God's will and have prevented ourselves from receiving what we need. God is willing to give us the desires of our hearts in greater measures than we can imagine, but many of those times when we sought God, we may have been our own hindrance. The scripture also states, "When you ask, you do not receive, because you ask with wrong motives, that you may spend what you get on your pleasures" (James 4:3). Wrong motives speak of inappropriate requests, which lead to rejection of our requests, even if those requests are in the form of a fast.

Illegitimate Fasting Leaves People Weary and Faint

"Then one of the soldiers told him, "Your father bound the army under a strict oath, saying, 'Cursed be anyone who eats food today!' That is why the men are faint" (1 Samuel 14:29–30).

Isaiah 40:31 states, "But they that wait upon The Lord shall renew their strength; they shall mount up with wings as eagles; they shall run, and not be weary; they shall run and not faint." To *wait*, in this context, is to render service as a "waiter," so to wait on God is to render service to Him. The waiter's service is self-sacrificing and not self-centered. To fast in order to avoid a curse or to fast in order to please yourself in something you desire is not service to God. The service that God desires of us is to "act justly" (with others), to love mercy (and show it to others) and to walk humbly with God. This means that service to God is about blessing others in selflessness as unto God. The army of Israel grew weary because they were not waiting on the Lord; they were waiting on Saul. They were not renewed in strength, even though the Lord placed His blessing of refreshment right under their noses.

God Does Not Respond to Illegitimate Fasting

"Saul said, "Let us go down and pursue the Philistines by night and plunder them till dawn, and let us not leave one of them alive." "Do whatever seems best to you," they replied. But the priest said, "Let us inquire of God here." So Saul asked God, "Shall I go down and pursue the Philistines? Will you give them into Israel's hand?" But God did not answer him that day" (1 Samuel 14:36–37).

It's funny how Saul was so hasty to call for a fast to avenge his enemy, but he was not mindful to pray and seek God for direction about how to defeat his enemies. This further exposes the misunderstanding Saul had concerning fasting and the lack of concern he had for knowing what God had to say. So when Saul finally asked the Lord for direction, the Lord did not reply. It wasn't because the Lord was upset that Saul forgot to ask for direction, and so He chose to be silent. Rather, I believe, He was being faithful to His Word—that anyone who treats fasting as an attempt to show God that he or she is deserving of God's power and assistance will not be heard.

I'd like to interject the definition, according to Merriam-Webster, of the word *illegitimate*: "Not sanctioned by law, or illegal." It indicates the absence of following the set standard or law that governs. In other words, with regard to Saul's fast, he did not follow God's standards for the sacrifice of fasting. He presented an illegitimate sacrifice to God, as Cain did, and the God who does not change rejected him and his sacrifice by not answering. I believe God saw that Cain's sacrifice came from a heart that had hatred for God's standards, which spread to hatred for his brother, which culminated in murder. I am not surprised that Saul was quick to kill his own son after fasting because he, just like Cain, offered his sacrifice with a hatred for God's standards. Saul rejected the true purpose for fasting when he made it about his own ambitions and not about for that which God established fasting. In doing this, he made his fast illegitimate, resulting in God's silence to his prayer.

Illegitimate Fasting Gives People a False Sense of Godliness

> Then Saul prayed to the Lord, the God of Israel, "Why have you not answered your servant today? If the fault is in me or my son Jonathan, respond with Urim, but if the men of Israel are at fault, respond with Thummim." Jonathan and Saul were taken by lot, and the men were cleared. Saul said, "Cast the lot between me and Jonathan my son." And Jonathan was taken. Then Saul said to Jonathan, "Tell me what you have done." So Jonathan told him, "I tasted a little honey with the end of my staff. And now I must die!" Saul said, "May God deal with me, be it ever so severely, if you do not die, Jonathan." (1 Samuel 14:41–44)

To understand the point I am about to make, let me first point out some things to consider. There were three violations recorded in the event between Saul, Jonathan, and the army. These violations were:

1. Saul's illegitimate fast for selfish ambitions; inconsideration of his army, and of God's purpose for fasting
2. Jonathan's violation of the oath under which the army was placed, by eating the honey they found (Though he unknowingly did this, he did break the oath.)
3. The army's eating meat with the blood still in it.

Of these three offenders, Saul and the army were offenders against God, but Jonathan was an ignorant offender of the senseless oath. When

Saul did not get an answer to his prayer, he assumed it was because someone broke the oath. So Saul sought the Lord to know who broke the oath. When the lots were cast, eventually Jonathan was identified as the culprit. But was it because of sin that the Lord singled out Jonathan? Let's give deeper consideration to this event; up to that moment, the Lord was using Jonathan, and Jonathan was obedient to the Lord's promptings. Even when he ate the honey, he was in the will of God, for the honey was prepared for the people to be refreshed. It was the illegitimate fast that forced the army to refrain from eating the honey, yet the same army broke God's law by eating meat with the blood still in it. Of these three offenses, at least one of them caused God to ignore Saul's prayer.

I like the commentary British theologian and biblical scholar Adam Clarke made on this matter. He wrote:

> The object of the inquiry most evidently was, "Who has gone contrary to the king's adjuration today?" The answer to that must be Jonathan. But was this a proof of the Divine displeasure against the man? By no means: the holy oracle told the truth, but neither that oracle nor the God who gave it fixed any blame upon Jonathan, and his own conscience acquits him. He seeks not pardon from God, because he is conscious he had not transgressed. But why did not God answer the priest that day? Because He did not think it proper to send the people by night in pursuit of the vanquished Philistines. Saul's motive was perfectly vindictive.

Had the people gone forward to fight the Philistines after sinning against the Lord by eating meat with the blood still in it, and had Saul continued without divine guidance because of his illegitimate fasting, then they most likely would not have seen victory that night. Jonathan and the armor-bearer would have been the only two who were in God's will at that time while the others would have been cut off from God's favor. The reason the Lord did not answer Saul's prayer was to express His disapproval of Saul's fast and the people's behavior and to use the conclusion of this matter to reveal that Jonathan was the only one who was walking in His will. Remember Isaiah stated, "Your fasting ends in quarreling and strife, and in striking each other with wicked fists. *You cannot fast as you do today and expect your voice to be heard on high*" (Isaiah 58:4).

God clearly stated that unanswered prayer is a result of illegitimate fasting. At the end of this great controversy we see that Saul wanted to kill Jonathan because he was singled out as the one who broke the oath. Saul thought he was righteous before God because he was fasting, but he was only being self-righteous and didn't even recognize that God as ignoring him because of his unrighteousness. The scripture states, "The Lord is far from the wicked, but he hears the prayer of the righteous" (Proverbs 15:29).

God would have answered Saul if he'd been righteous, but God did not answer because Saul's fast was to strike with the fist of wickedness. We even see this wickedness in the way he hastily sentenced Jonathan to death. Proverbs 15:28 states, "The heart of the righteous weighs its answers, but the mouth of the wicked gushes evil." Saul did not weigh his answer, for if he had, he would have seen that there was more to the situation than meets the eye. Yet we see God's mercy on Jonathan by keeping him from death. Proverbs 26:2 states, "Like a fluttering sparrow or a darting swallow, an undeserved curse does not come to rest." God ensured that Saul's curse did not land on Jonathan, and in doing so, God showed that He was on Jonathan's side.

This makes it easier to understand why illegitimate fasting gives a false sense of godliness. Saul was oblivious to his state with God when he entered into that illegitimate fast. Because he was fasting, he assumed that it placed him in good standing with God. So when the time came to see who really sinned, he didn't have a clue. He was willing to kill his own son immediately after a fast! This shows that when people do not understand what fasting is about, they treat it as a deed that makes them righteous, giving them a false sense of holiness. Those who think this way fast and then fight with others during and after they fast. But if they realized that fasting is an expression of love in the form of self-sacrifice, it would be difficult to see harm come to others. After all, *others* should be the prime reason why you fast.

Desperate Fasting Can Be Illegitimate Fasting

"The Philistines assembled and came and set up camp at Shunem, while Saul gathered all Israel and set up camp at Gilboa. When Saul saw the Philistine army, he was afraid; terror filled his heart. He inquired of the Lord, but the Lord did not answer him by dreams or Urim or prophets. Saul then said to his attendants, "Find me a woman who is a medium, so I may go and inquire of her." "There is one in Endor," they said" (1 Samuel 28:4–7).

When I refer to desperate fasting, I am not speaking of someone who is desperately pursuing intimacy with God, desperately desiring to know His ways, and zealously giving himself or herself for God's service. Rather, I am referring to someone's attempts to use fasting to show God that he or she is desperately seeking answers. This type of fasting I also categorize as illegitimate fasting. To fast in this manner is to add a "fleshy" element to your fast—not desperation but manipulation. In desperation, many have fasted with the hope that God would see how desperate they are and grant them what they desire. But that is not how fasting works. God has clearly identified in His Word the purpose for fasting; it is the sacrifice one makes with his or her own body for the sake of others and for the glory of God.

Saul used fasting as a desperate attempt to get God to answer his question about a battle between the Israelites and the Philistines. But fasting was not the only thing for which Saul tried to get a response from God. The scripture records that he tried dreams, the Urim, the prophets, and then fasting, but none of them worked. Trying one option after another was a clear sign of Saul's desperation, and because he did not get an answer from God, I can only imagine that it led to frustration. Out of desperation, he eventually sought a medium to speak to the dead while he fasted. I wonder if Saul thought because he was attempting to speak to Samuel that it would be okay. He must have thought that none of the other prophets was as good a prophet as Samuel. But to seek counsel from the dead is to turn completely away from God, for God is God of the living and not the dead.

The scripture states, "I am the God of Abraham, the God of Isaac, and the God of Jacob. He is not the God of the dead but of the living" (Matthew 22:32). It is also recorded in scripture: "The mind governed by the flesh is death, but the mind governed by the Spirit is life and peace"

(Romans 8:6). To seek the dead is synonymous to pursuing the mind governed by the flesh. So Saul's efforts to seek counsel from the dead symbolize someone's trying to find answers from within himself or herself and not God while fasting. They attempted to conjure up an answer for themselves and sought the dead when they felt the Lord was not answering. But as I mentioned earlier, God is not the God of the dead.

The apostle Paul spoke to the Galatians about this issue when he wrote, "Are you so foolish? After beginning by means of the Spirit, are you now trying to finish by means of the flesh?" (Galatians 3:3). Paul was warning the believers in Galatia not to go back to living from the strength of the flesh because it never profited them in the first place. Saul did the very same thing. He started out as one anointed by God and ended up as one who followed his feelings.

Let's be careful that we do not go back to "means of the flesh" when we fast. Desperation for attention does not reflect the maturity that is displayed in trusting God and believing His Word. Desperation and manipulation are foxes that spoil a good thing, like fasting. So with this understanding, "Catch for us the foxes, the little foxes that ruin the vineyards ... " (Song of Solomon 2:15).

Desperate Fasting Is an Attempt to Manipulate God

Hidden in Saul's desperate attempts to get God to answer was a spirit of manipulation. When Saul realized that manipulation didn't work— manipulation will never get us anywhere with God—he went a step further and engaged in witchcraft. Saul was not merely attempting to talk to a dead prophet; he was seeking demonic assistance for answers. We can see from Saul's life how he went from living by his own opinions, to being influenced by an evil spirit, to pursuing evil spirits for assistance.

I remember having a conversation with my sister Clara about manipulation being associated with witchcraft. She said that demons manipulate people, and when we encounter someone who is manipulative, there is a demonic spirit of manipulation behind that behavior. To fast in order to persuade God to answer you is manipulation, and this behavior actually stems directly from the demonic.

Saul had been manipulative before when he made his army take an oath to fast by cursing anyone who would not fast. He also attempted to manipulate Samuel into going with him after he disobeyed God's command to destroy the Amalekites. Through such events as these, he opened the door for the spirit of manipulation, and before you know it, that spirit led him to manipulate David to marry his daughter and to manipulate Jonathan to bring David to the banquet so he could kill him. He even manipulated Doeg the Edomite to kill the eighty-five priests of the Lord in Nob.

In essence, the spirit of manipulation seeks opportunity to snuff out the anointing or the anointed ones. This is why fasting as a desperate attempt to sway God is to be avoided at all costs, lest we open the door for a spirit of manipulation to enter our lives. Remember that when the Spirit left Saul after he attempted to manipulate the man of God, an evil spirit from the Lord attached itself to Saul. How much more trouble could we enter into if we attempted to manipulate God?

Desperation Removes Faith from Fasting

"When I shut up the heavens so that there is no rain, or command locusts to devour the land or send a plague among my people, if my people, who are called by my name, will humble themselves and pray and seek my face and turn from their wicked ways, then I will hear from heaven, and I will forgive their sin and will heal their land" (2 Chronicles 7:13–14). The above scripture states, "If my people will ..." The instructions that follow those four words describe God's strict requirements that will guarantee His response. This command does not suggest there are options, and fasting is one of them. Instead, it refers to fasting as the solution to getting God's ear—period! This means fasting is not to be a last resort but the intentional sacrificing of your life, as prompted by the Holy Spirit.

I believe Saul was fasting while he was seeking a medium because the scripture states,

> Immediately Saul fell full length on the ground, filled with fear because of Samuel's words. His strength was gone, for he had eaten nothing all that day and all that night. When the woman came to Saul and saw that he was

greatly shaken, she said, "Look, your servant has obeyed
you. I took my life in my hands and did what you told me
to do. Now please listen to your servant and let me give
you some food so you may eat and have the strength to go
on your way. "He refused and said, "I will not eat. "But his
men joined the woman in urging him, and he listened to
them. He got up from the ground and sat on the couch.
The woman had a fattened calf at the house, which she
butchered at once. She took some flour, kneaded it and
baked bread without yeast. Then she set it before Saul and
his men, and they ate. That same night they got up and
left. (1 Samuel 28:20–25)

Saul was fasting when he approached the medium, but this was a fast
of desperation and not one of concern for God's people.

Let's take a closer look at Saul's fast, and we will see how desperate
fasting can equate to illegitimate fasting. Saul fasted when he could not
get an answer from God about the battle that he was about to enter, but it
was only out of desperation for an answer. This means desperate fasting is
done in times of trouble merely to get out of trouble. Saul sought answers
from God through prayer, dreams, prophets, fasting, and finally through
a medium. This made fasting an option. So desperate fasting involves
considering God and fasting as merely an option and not a sure solution to
having God's ear. Since Saul was more concerned about an answer than he
was about pleasing God, in his mind even ungodly means were permitted.

Desperate fasting allows for using ungodly means to expect godly
answers; it involves treating God as one who can be manipulated by our
frantic behavior and pretentious concerns in times of desperation. Just as
Saul easily broke his fast at the word of the woman, desperate fasting is
soul-driven, and the those fasting are easily manipulated by the opinions
of others during their fasts. This removes the characteristic of a sacrifice
from the fast and treats the fast as a display instead of the true humbling
of ourselves before God. And finally, desperate fasting is never about
mercy or sorrowful repentance but about getting out of a jam. Saul never
once showed any concern about the army or Israel but only about himself.
This made the answer from the encounter with Samuel fitting, because

Samuel said, "This day you and your sons shall be with me in the grave" (1 Samuel 28:19).

So we have looked at the life of King Saul as an example of one whose fast was illegitimate and resulted in God's silence, confusion, missed opportunities, weariness, and even rebellion.

Now let's look at King David and the fast that he offered unto God. I will use his fast to describe what God considers legitimate fasting. In this fast we will find wonderful treasures that will add great value to our lives and to the fast that we offer unto God.

Legitimate Fasting—Is There Not a Cause?

This is where the joy begins. Let's see what kinds of fasts pleased God and in what way they pleased Him. These are legitimate fasts because they were according to the standards that God prescribed. In them, we will find love and the sacrificing of himself unto God for others. We also will find a dependency on God for answers and a reluctance to do things without His approval. I appreciated the lessons from King Saul that tell me what to avoid, but I am always filled with excitement to read of King David and learn what I can do that pleases God. One thing that stands out in David's life is the tendency to see the cause and the necessity to put his life on the line to make a difference. David's stand against Goliath was not the only time David saw a cause. Scripture records other moments when David fasted for this reason. This sets David apart from his predecessor Saul, who seemed not to see the cause to sacrifice in his own life, even when it was staring him in the face.

My prayer is that a fire will begin to burn within you as you see that your life is better lived when you use it as a sacrifice. There is no greater use of your life than to put it on the line. One of the ways of doing that is in fasting for a cause.

Legitimate Fasting—Because You Care

"Then they all came and urged David to eat something while it was still day; but David took an oath, saying, "May God deal with me, be it ever so severely, if I taste bread or anything else before the sun sets!" (2 Samuel 3:35).

There is that oath again, but this time it's different. Unlike Saul, who placed a curse on the people if they didn't fast, David placed a curse on himself if he didn't fast. Here's the circumstance that builds up to David's oath: one day Joab, captain of David's army, and Abner, captain of Isbosheth's army (that is, Saul's son) had their men fight each other in a fair match, twelve men each. Joab's men defeated Abner's men, and as the fight exploded into a battle, Joab's men began to chase after Abner's. In that battle, Abner killed Joab's younger brother after he refused to stop chasing him, although Abner had pleaded with him to leave him alone.

After some time passed and Abner's allegiance changed from Isbosheth's to David's—immediately after Abner had just had a peaceful meeting with David to help him gain the kingdom of Israel—Joab sent for Abner and pretended to be at peace with him. He then killed Abner for killing his younger brother. When David heard of this, he rebuked Joab and commanded the people to mourn, but he fasted. Now the question is, why did David fast?

It would not be a stretch to say it was a ritual, for fasting after the death of someone was not unheard of. But what made this customary fast legitimate was the meaning for fasting during that time. David did not simply see what Joab did as a needed avenging of blood. Instead, he saw evil done among his men and sought God's mercy on behalf of the nation, so that God would not bring judgment and destruction for the wrongful avenging of blood. In other words, David cared about the negative impact Joab's sin could have on the nation. He cared that leaders in the nation disobeyed God's word which would cause a curse upon the land. Because David cared about these things, he saw the cause for fasting.

As stated in the proverb, "There are six things the Lord hates, seven that are detestable to him: haughty eyes, a lying tongue, *hands that shed innocent blood, a heart that devises wicked schemes, feet that are quick to rush into evil*, a false witness who pours out lies and a person who stirs up conflict in the community" (Proverbs 6:16–19, emphasis added). Though Abner killed Joab's brother in a battle, it was not right for Joab to kill Abner, especially in a time of peace. David recognized this wrong and resorted to fasting. David did not resort to more violence by attempting to kill Joab, for this would lead to much more bloodshed—he was the captain of the army with many men who were probably very loyal to him. So David put all these things into God's hands by refraining from perpetuating the avenging of blood, and he fasted for God's mercy for the wrongful killing. This was not the only reason why David fasted, for David also recognized that Israel was in some way crippled because of the loss of a great man like Abner.

Abner's character showed integrity and honor, while Joab's character included murderous tendencies. So David fasted before the Lord so that God would give grace to Israel in the midst of such a loss. The scripture records David's words in this way: "Then King David said to his officials, "Don't you realize that a great commander has fallen today in Israel? And even though I am the anointed king, these two sons of Zeruiah—Joab and Abishai—are too strong for me to control. So may the Lord repay these evil men for their evil deeds" (2 Samuel 3:38–39). So David's fast was legitimate fasting; he did not oppress others but was willing to put his own stomach on the line for others. He recognized the evil that would have brought a curse upon the land and became a humble sacrifice so that his lament could be heard on high to remove the potential curse. David saw the cause for fasting because he cared for God's people.

Legitimate Fasting—An Effective Response to Evil Deeds

From David's example, we see that whenever there is evil done that would ultimately affect others, fasting before the Lord and mourning over the matter is pleasing to God. It's interesting to note that soon after these events we see that God allowed David to rule over the nation of Israel. In spite of the event with Joab and Abner, God still favored David and used David to make a difference for good in the land and to bless God's people. And who better to be used to bless others than the one who has others on his mind and is willing to fast so that God would be gracious to them? David was not being hypocritical or ritualistic when he fasted after Abner's death. He understood the purpose for fasting and implemented it as the appropriate response for evil around him. Acting in love for the people, he did not force the people to fast but instead forced them to mourn. He did this because fasting must begin with a heart of love for God and his people and not out of compulsion.

Today we see a lot of injustice and evil in the world, just as David did in his time. As the people of God, we must not just sit and talk about it. We know that evil deeds are a result of sin, and the answer to the sin problem in the world is love. As an answer to the sin problem of the world, God sent His Son to pour out love in the world. Love saves the world from sin; it truly covers a multitude of sins. The scripture states, "Because of the increase of wickedness, the love of most will grow cold, but the one who stands firm to the end will be saved" (Matthew 24:12–13). The King James Version uses the words "where sin abounds" in place of "because of the increase of wickedness." When sin is abounding or prevalent, the natural response is for people to reduce the love they show. But a love that grows cold is not the answer to abounding sin and wickedness. Love is the answer, as the scripture states: "Above all, love each other deeply, because love covers over a multitude of sins" (1 Peter 4:8). The love sacrifice of fasting can save the sinful world around you. It is the highest God-ordained response from His people to address the evil around them.

Legitimate Fasting—"Out of Concern for the Anointing

Fasting is the appropriate response if or when we see an anointed leader stumble or fall. When Saul and his sons died, David and the people fasted, and David wept and lamented because of the loss and what it meant to Israel. Though Saul chased David like a dog to kill him, Saul's death and the death of his sons brought sorrow to David because he saw Saul's death as the death of the Lord's anointed. Both Saul and the one who would be his best successor died in the same battle—king and prince. Fasting, as David did in this situation, shows the genuine concern David had for the people of his nation. Let's take a lesson from David here. Whenever we see people who are great spiritual leaders fall in our community, state, or nation, we should think of fasting for that leader and the people who are affected by the fall of such a great leader, who once carried the anointing. Let us refrain from gossiping and finger-pointing and instead become those who would care about the impact the fall could have on others. Be concerned about what the loss of an anointed one means to the nation, community, or church. Recognize the cause, and truly stand in the gap. First Chronicles 7:14 implies that if calamity has been sent to a church, community, state, or nation, and if God's people who are called by His name care enough to fast and cry out to God on their behalf, then He will bring healing there.

Legitimate Fasting—Quietly Fast and Publicly Lament

There are two ways to show obvious love when we fast: one is through silent fasting and the other is through public lamentation. This may seem contradictory, in that fasting and lamenting go hand in hand, but allow me to explain.

Jesus said, "When you fast, do not look somber as the hypocrites do, for they disfigure their faces to show others they are fasting. Truly I tell you, they have received their reward in full. But when you fast, put oil on your head and wash your face, so that it will not be obvious to others that you are fasting, but only to your Father, who is unseen; and your Father, who sees what is done in secret, will reward you" (Matthew 6:16–18). This scripture speaks of the silence we must display to others when we fast. Because fasting is a love gift, for the gift to be genuine it requires that you be silent about it to others. Sounding the trumpet to others about your time of fasting tells God that your concern is not about others but about your pride. Sounding a trumpet about your fast is an attempt to use your fast as a show of piety and holiness. In a sense, publicizing your fast is like publicizing your gift, making the right hand know what the left hand is doing while giving. This is not a true generosity, nor is it a genuine gift. Proverbs speak of those who appear to be generous but who are not even concerned about you. It states, "Don't eat with people who are stingy; don't desire their delicacies. They are always thinking about how much it costs. *"Eat and drink,"* they say, *but they don't mean it.* You will throw up what little you've eaten, and your compliments will be wasted" (Proverbs 23:6–8, NLT, emphasis added).

Jesus warned us about being the stingy person who claims to be generous and concerned while calculating how we would benefit from our so-called generosity. For this reason, when we fast, to truly express our love for the ones for whom we fast, we must release the gift of fasting without seeking any praise for ourselves in return. This is the true definition of a gift. When David fasted after Abner died, it was done silently unto the Lord, so that the Lord, who saw in secret, would reward him by blessing Israel. The people for whom he fasted could receive the genuine gift out of true generosity and experience the merciful blessings of God. The people were so oblivious of David's fast that they brought him food, and it was then that they found out he was fasting.

With regard to lamenting, let's again look at what David did when he fasted. Though David did not let Israel know that he was fasting for them, he did let them know that he was mourning, and he even commanded them to mourn. In this way, David fasted and lamented for Saul, Jonathan, and even Abner. Lamenting is an expression of a sorrowful emotion, and making this expression public is no sin. Sorrow ought to be the emotion we express when we fast out of concern for the cause. As I mentioned previously about David, he saw a cause, and it drove him to fast and lament. If we remain silent about causes, people become callous. Callousness is the worldly response to wickedness, as we saw in the scripture mentioned previously: "Because of the increase of wickedness, the love of most will grow cold." But the expressions of caring and concern through lamentation breaks the callous heart. Causes such as the loss of the nation's leaders or the disregard for God's law led David to public, sorrowful laments. The scriptures record David's lamentations when he fasted after Saul and Abner died. When Saul died, David mourned and lamented before the Lord to express the sorrow in his heart concerning Israel's facing the great loss of their leader. His lamentation was not to please the men who were around him; it was to help them understand what truly happened so they might also express sorrow so that their hearts would not become callous about the evil and loss.

Jesus gave witness to the wisdom of this type of lamentation when He said, "Blessed are those who mourn, for they will be comforted" (Matthew 5:4). Lamentation ought to be the response we have whenever we see something prevailing around us that is harmful to others. Lamentation like this gives witness to our concern for the affairs around us. Even Jesus lamented when He saw that Jerusalem was not responding to His message. He said, "Jerusalem, Jerusalem, you who kill the prophets and stone those sent to you, how often I have longed to gather your children together, as a hen gathers her chicks under her wings, and you were not willing" (Matthew 23:37). Lamentation comes from a heart of love; it is an expression of concern for the need of righteousness when it is not there. It is a cry that represents the pain in your heart over prevailing evil. Because lamentation is an expression of love, it is always present when you truly fast. Lamenting must be broadcast so that people can know there is a cause, and who better to lament than those who are willing to die to see a change come about?

Look at the lament David made after Saul's death. David said, "A gazelle lies slain on your heights, Israel. How the mighty have fallen! "Tell it not in Gath, proclaim it not in the streets of Ashkelon, lest the daughters of the Philistines be glad, lest the daughters of the uncircumcised rejoice" (2 Samuel 1:19–20). Lamentations counteract the spreading of evil words. If the righteous do not speak in lamentation about the evil, then the evil words will be propagated. Consider David's response to Abner's death. Though Abner was recently on the opposing team, when Joab killed him in revenge, David mourned and lamented, saying, "Should Abner have died as the lawless die? Your hands were not bound, your feet were not fettered. You fell as one falls before the wicked" (2 Samuel 3:33–34). These lamentations ought to make others consider what is happening around them. This part of fasting must be public.

If we look closer at David's lamentation, we will see that David was even more concerned about the people who were still alive, though they did not know it. He explained to them later on that "a great man died and the wicked ones still lived." This means that Abner, who was a great man, could have been one of their rulers, but instead the wicked were ruling. When David saw that great men like Joab, the commander of the army, and Abishai, one of David's great military leaders, were resorting to wicked ways, he knew the trouble that could fall on Israel, so he fasted and lamented. Look at the comparison David made between Joab, Abishai, and Abner. He said, "Then the king said to his men, *Do you not realize that a commander and a great man has fallen in Israel this day?* And today, though I am the anointed king, I am weak, and these sons of Zeruiah are too strong for me. *May the Lord repay the evildoer according to his evil deeds!*" (2 Samuel 3:38–39, emphasis added). David referred to Abner as a great man, but he referred to Joab and his brother as evildoers. Sadly, the great man died, while the evildoers lived. In Proverbs, it states, "When the righteous are in authority, the people rejoice: *but when the wicked beareth rule, the people mourn*" (Proverbs 29:2 KJV, emphasis added). Whenever we see innocent people dying while the evildoers live, we must fast and lament. As the proverb states, "when the wicked rule, we must mourn," so that God will be merciful and the people will not grow callous toward wickedness in the land.

CHAPTER 3

Fasting Reveals God's Mercies

There are scriptures in the Bible that tell us the Lord repented. Due to misunderstanding the context, it may have been misinterpreted. Because we have become familiar with the term *repent* in relation to our sins, wherever we see the phrase "God repented," we have the tendency to apply the commonly known meaning of the word. Repentance from God's perspective is not the same as it is from a human perspective. For us, repentance is turning away from sinful living and to a holy life, but for God, repentance is changing His response to us. Because God does not ever need to change His mind as we do when we turn from sin, when it is written that God repented, it means that He turned from one legitimate outcome to a desired outcome, or vice versa. He turned from justice (the legitimate outcome) to mercy (His desired outcome), or vice versa. I refer to God's desired outcome as mercy because the scripture states, "It is of the Lord's mercies that we are not consumed, because His compassions fail not. They [that is, His mercies] are new every morning: great is Thy faithfulness" (Lamentations 3:22–23 KJV).

It is "His mercies that are made new every morning," not "His judgments are made new every morning." This is why I believe that mercy is God's preferred outcome. Just as God used love to covers a multitude of sins, He desires mercy to overcome judgments. Again the scripture speaks about mercy and sacrifice in this way (Jesus saying to the Pharisees): "But go and learn what this means: 'I desire mercy, not sacrifice.' For I have not come to call the righteous, but sinners" (Matthew 9:13, referring to Hosea 6:6). The sacrifice that Jesus is referring to in this scripture is an act or deed

done in an effort to please God while justifying self. God does not desire
acts or deeds done in an effort to justify yourself. He desires obedience
that results in acts and deeds done in an effort to please Him. This means
the concept of sacrificing is not discarded, but God evaluates the type of
sacrifice and purpose for the sacrifice.

The scripture speaks about sacrifice in this way: "Therefore when
Christ came into the world, He said: Sacrifice and offering You did not
desire, but a body You prepared for Me; with burnt offerings and sin
offerings you were not pleased. Then I said, Here I am—it is written
about me in the scroll—I have come to do Your will, My God" (Hebrews
10:5–7, referring to Psalm 40:6). It was the will of God that Jesus become
a sacrifice for our sins, to ask for God's mercy on our behalf. So sacrificing
was not discarded, but the type of sacrifice that pleased God was clarified.
I believe that we are also living sacrifices prepared to express God's mercy
and not created merely for the purpose of physical sacrifices, as many may
think. This is why understanding fasting is so important for the believer
because the sacrifice of fasting makes us eligible to seek God for mercy on
behalf of others.

Fasting Qualifies You to Cry for God to Repent

> But Moses sought the favor of the LORD his God. "LORD,"
> he said, "why should your anger burn against your people,
> whom you brought out of Egypt with great power and
> a mighty hand? Why should the Egyptians say, 'It was
> with evil intent that he brought them out, to kill them
> in the mountains and to wipe them off the face of the
> earth'? Turn from your fierce anger; relent and do not
> bring disaster on your people. Remember your servants
> Abraham, Isaac and Israel, to whom you swore by your
> own self: 'I will make your descendants as numerous as
> the stars in the sky and I will give your descendants all
> this land I promised them, and it will be their inheritance
> forever.'" Then the LORD relented and did not bring the
> disaster he had threatened. (Exodus 32:11–14)

The people of Israel had recently experienced God's speaking from a burning mountain, telling them the Ten Commandments. When they heard this, they were afraid of God and asked for a mediator—a priest, in a sense. God granted them what they wanted and told Moses to come up to the mountain to receive the full commandments. Moses spent forty days and nights (maybe more) on the mountain, and the people started wondering if something had happened to him and that he would not come back. So they approached Aaron and said he should make a god to lead them out of the wilderness. Aaron did, and the people worshiped the image that Aaron made. Meanwhile, God told Moses, who was still up the mountain, that the people were sinning against God and that He was planning to destroy them. To destroy the people would have been a just reward for blatantly disobeying God's command, which He'd recently given to them. (We must remember that the more direct the command, the greater the consequences are for disobeying them.)

God came on the mountain and displayed His greatness. He spoke to them Himself, audibly from the mountain, and all the people heard it. It would have taken a lot to disbelieve that the Lord had just spoken, yet the people did not regard the words of the Lord, and they didn't fear Him as He is to be feared. And so they sinned against Him by making the golden image of God in the form of a creature the Lord made on earth. Moses pleaded for their lives, and the scriptures states, "*The Lord repented of the evil* which He thought to do unto His people" (Exodus 32:14 KJV, emphasis added). The evil spoken of here is the just judgment God had in mind for the people's disobedience. That just judgment was called evil; this tells me that God so desires mercy that even just judgment, when compared to His mercy, appears as evil.

I believe that God sought an opportunity in Moses to have mercy as an outcome. What I mean is, God prepared Moses to be a sacrifice and led him to fast while he was on the mountain. And when the people sinned, God revealed the judgment for their sin to Moses. When He did this, Moses, who was already seeking the best interests of the people, was eligible to cry out for mercy on behalf of the people. The scripture records that the Lord repented. This again leads me to that well-known scripture that states, "If my people, who are called by my name, will humble themselves and pray and seek my face and turn from their wicked ways, then I will

hear from heaven, and I will forgive their sin and will heal their land"
(2 Chronicles 7:14). God's people can be eligible to cry out for mercy on
behalf of their family members, neighbors, coworkers, and so on. And the
cry for mercy requires that someone stand in the gap on behalf of another.
This is why fasting is so important to God, because through it, He brings
about His desired end, which is mercy.

Fasting Is the Life's Cry for Mercy

"You have come to Jesus, the one who mediates the new covenant
between God and people, and to the sprinkled blood, which speaks of
forgiveness instead of crying out for vengeance like the blood of Abel"
(Hebrews 12:24 NLT).

The act of fasting is dying to our appetite and to intentionally abstain
from the food that is used to keep us alive. This may sound like a suicidal
tendency, but the purpose of the fast gives it a proper perspective. As Jesus
said, "No one can take my life from me. *I sacrifice it voluntarily.* For I have
the authority to lay it down when I want to and also to take it up again.
For this is what my Father has commanded" (John 10:18 NLT, emphasis
added). This sounds like fasting to me—the authority to lay down my life
when I want and to also take it back up again. Just as Jesus had a purpose
for laying down His life, so is our purpose similar. He died for the sins of
the world so that He might stand as an advocate for all who repent. While
on the cross He cried for mercy on their behalf. "Jesus said, 'Father, forgive
them, for they do not know what they are doing'" (Luke 23:34).

We fast and die to our desires for food so that we can be eligible to cry
for mercy for others in the same way Jesus did. One of the problems that
judgmental people have is that they believe people know what is right, yet
they do the wrong. But if we truly consider what it means to know, we
would not be that way. Knowing is like seeing, and one who sees does not
stumble while it is day. But someone who is blind cannot see, so although it
is day, the person does not know what he or she is doing. The mercy of God
is to forgive people for their blindness and to give them sight. This is why
we also must desire to become eligible to cry out, "Father, forgive them,
for they do not know what they are doing." And as the Father accepted

Jesus's act of becoming a sacrifice for all, in the same way God will accept our living sacrifice of fasting on behalf of others.

Fasting for mercy also can be seen from another perspective. The scriptures speak of forgiveness in this manner: "In fact, the law requires that nearly everything be cleansed with blood, and without the shedding of blood there is no forgiveness" (Hebrew 9:22). The shedding of blood means death, so death is the requirement for cleansing, according to the law of God, because as the scripture states, "Without the shedding of blood there is no forgiveness." This means that sin equals death, and forgiveness requires death. Yet another way to see it is to say, death cancels sin. This means that our dying to self on behalf of others (which is the greatest love) can cancel sins. The scriptures states, "Above all, love each other deeply, because love covers over a multitude of sins" (1 Peter 4:8). And we are called to love as God loves. John wrote, "Dear friends, let us love one another, for love comes from God. Everyone who loves has been born of God and knows God" (1 John 4:7).

If we are children of God, we are called to love as God loved. God loved us from the very beginning and expressed it by giving us His breath, showing us His mercies, giving us His laws, sending His Son to die for us, and even giving us His Holy Spirit. All these acts of love were not warranted but are gifts to us. In this way, our fasting for the sake of others must be as gifts to them at our expense. The gift of everlasting life was given to us by God the Father through Jesus. In the same way, the freedom from bondage of all sorts that can be broken from people's lives must be given to them as a gift from God, through us when we fast. The apostle Paul wrote about this in Romans and stated it this way: "For the wages of sin is death, *but the gift of God is eternal life* in Christ Jesus our Lord" (Romans 6:23, emphasis added). Another way to say this is that the payment for sin is the laying down of a life, or the payment for sin is love expressed through mercy. As God's children, we must be eager to facilitate our Father's desires by becoming agents of mercy, by way of submission through fasting.

The need to lay down our lives for others is only necessary when there is transgression and a requirement for God's justice. In laying down our lives in fasting, we join with God's desire to see others turn and live. As it is written in Ezekiel, "Do I take any pleasure in the death of the wicked?

declares the Sovereign LORD. Rather, am I not pleased when they turn from their ways and live?" (Ezekiel 18:23). God searches the land for someone to stand in the gap; that is, a person who is willing to put aside his or her own food and satisfactions to intercede for another. Remember, God looks for ways to bless the people of the earth, and He does it through people who are willing to leave their lives, their fathers' houses and kindred, even their glory, and go to a place where they can receive instructions from the Lord that brings about a blessing for many. God looks for someone to bring restoration by building up broken-down walls. As He said again in Ezekiel, "I looked for someone among them who would build up the wall and stand before me in the gap on behalf of the land so I would not have to destroy it, but I found no one" (Ezekiel 22:30). The Lord looks for ways to turn from destroying; this is the Lord's repentance.

In most cases, walls are built to protect the occupants of a property from trespassers. The walls of a house or building is used to provide safety and privacy to the people inside. But when the walls are broken-down, the safety, and privacy of the occupants are gone. The devil is a wicked trespasser and he seeks areas that are broken-down in our understanding and belief so that he might enter in to harm the occupants. Broken-down walls means there are missing parts of the wall that provides a means for the trespasser to slip by and to wreak havoc. Anyone who misunderstands the truth, or do not know the truth are vulnerable to trespassers who bring in lies to confuse and destroy. For this reason, whenever there is a breaches in their wall, it should be quickly repaired. God look for people who would partner with Him in the task of being equip to repair broken-down walls. Sadly, in Ezekiel's day God looked and found none.

Fasting is a God given tool that we can use to repair broken-down walls. It is written in the book of Isaiah,

> Is not this the fast that I have chosen? To loose the bands
> of wickedness, to undo the heavy burdens, and to let the
> oppressed go free, and that ye break every yoke? Is it not
> to deal thy bread to the hungry, and that thou bring the
> poor that are cast out to thy house? when thou seest the
> naked, that thou cover him; and that thou hide not thyself
> from thine own flesh?.....And they that shall be of thee

shall build the old waste places; thou shalt raise up the foundations of many generations, and *thou shalt be called the Repairer of the Breach*, the Restorer of Paths to dwell in." (Isaiah 58:6–7, 12 KJV)

Fasting God's way can empower us to become a repairer of breaches, that is broken-down walls. This means that when we fast God's way we can stand in the gap to get the missing truths that others need to repair their misunderstanding of the truth. Through fasting God can show mercy by repairing broken down understanding of the truth. God prefers to do this instead of giving unbelievers the judgment they deserve because of their misunderstanding and unbelief.

Fasting Prior to God's Judgments Results in Restoration

"His attendants asked him, "Why are you acting this way? While the child was alive, you fasted and wept, but now that the child is dead, you get up and eat!" He answered, "While the child was still alive, I fasted and wept. I thought, 'Who knows? The Lord may be gracious to me and let the child live.' But now that he is dead, why should I go on fasting? Can I bring him back again? I will go to him, but he will not return to me" (2 Samuel 12:21–23).

The above passage of scripture is about David's fast so that God might turn from the judgment He pronounced and allow his son to live. But God took David's son to be with Him because that was the wisdom of God for restoration because the boy was born out of adultery and in the midst of murder. This would have caused wicked people to speak incorrectly about God's goodness and righteousness. Please don't think that fasting didn't work here because it did. Fasting is about restoration and not just getting what we want as an outcome. With regard to God's taking the life of David's son, let's not be too hasty to judge God with evil. Look at what the Lord told Jeroboam about his son, who was sick: "As for you, go back home. When you set foot in your city, the boy will die. All Israel will mourn for him and bury him. He is the only one belonging to Jeroboam who will be buried, because he is the only one in the house of Jeroboam in whom the LORD God of Israel has found anything good." (1 Kings 14:12–13).

Here we see a child die, though it was the father who was disobedient to God's commands. Notice that God said the boy was the only one with whom He found anything good. I believe the reason God removed Jeroboam's son was not to punish Jeroboam but to show a sign of His willingness to preserve future generations from contaminating what is good by perpetuating iniquity. The same thing happened with David and his son. The Lord removed David's son not as a judgment to David but to prevent the perpetuation of iniquity. I am not certain if David understood or realized that was what the Lord was doing. Yet he said, "I will go to him." This statement could imply that David knew his son had been taken to a better place that he, David, would one day want to be. And in the end, God was not treated with contempt by those who would say God was in favor of David's sinful actions with Bathsheba.

When there is fasting before there is judgment, then there is hope for restoration. Fasting is a medium through which God brings mercy. Mercy must come before the time of judgment for judgment to be overcome. "Do I take any pleasure in the death of the wicked? declares the Sovereign LORD. Rather, am I not pleased when they turn from their ways and live?" (Ezekiel 18:23). This scripture in Ezekiel refers to God's desire to restore before the time of judgment. In His wisdom, God made the restoration process depend greatly on an object's capability to be broken before restoration can occur.

Anyone who fasts the way God has chosen has become an object of brokenness before the Lord. This brokenness is not for destruction but for repairing, even though it involves momentary breaking and crushing. But this crushing pleases God, as Isaiah testified :"Yet it was the LORD's will to crush Him [that is Jesus] and cause Him to suffer, and though the LORD makes His life an offering for sin, He will see His offspring and prolong His days, and the will of the LORD will prosper in His hand. After He has suffered, He will see the light of life and be satisfied; by His knowledge my righteous servant will justify many, and He will bear their iniquities" (Isaiah 53:10). Just as the Father was pleased to crush Jesus and cause Him to suffer, the Father is pleased that we are crushed and made to suffer. For it was the crushing and suffering of Jesus that resulted in the restoration of the broken relationship individuals had with God. It was through Jesus's suffering that the yokes of sin were removed from our necks so that the scripture holds true: "For sin shall no longer be your master, because you are not under the law, but under grace" (Romans 6:14). Yet the purpose of His suffering was so that He would become an offering for our sins in the same way we must become living sacrifices unto God.

The apostle Paul wrote, "Therefore, I urge you, brothers and sisters, in view of God's mercy, to offer your bodies as a living sacrifice, holy and pleasing to God—this is your true and proper worship" (Romans 12:1). This scripture says "your bodies." This coincides with presenting your bodies to be an offering in fasting on behalf of others, and this is considered a reasonable service. This is because of what Jesus said, as written in the Gospel of Matthew: "Then Jesus said to his disciples, "Whoever wants to be my disciple must deny themselves and take up their cross and follow me" (Matthew 16:24). To "come after" speaks of one who follows what someone else does or did. To be a follower of Jesus, we must be prepared to live a life of death for others. In other words, as Jesus was crushed, so we will be crushed for the will of the Father. When we are crushed and broken before the Lord in fasting, we are used to restore and to remove yokes. And as it was said about Jesus concerning His obedience unto death, it will be said about us: "For just as through the disobedience of the one man the many were made sinners, so also through the obedience of the one man the many will be made righteous" (Romans 5:19). Through our obedience unto death, in this case referring to fasting, we will be used by God in the restoration of many lives.

CHAPTER 4

Fasting for Instructions to Build

Throughout the scriptures, any reference to forty-day fasting has one thing in common with all of the others, which is that they all occurred before the building or rebuilding of something great. It seems as though God used forty-day fasting as a foundational ingredient for the building of character and the establishment or reestablishment of ministries. The main thing received during such a fast was instruction for building. I cannot tell you why, God in His wisdom, made forty days as a time frame, but during that period God sanctifies and purifies the vessels that He intends to use to manifest His will. The Lord showed me five keys about forty-day fasting through the events of fasting in Moses's time. (See Deuteronomy 9.) These five keys are as follows:

1. When on a forty-day fast, we must abide in the mountain until we receive what God wants to give us.
2. When on a forty-day fast, God gives us table of the covenant.
3. When on a forty-day fast, we will enter into God's glory cloud.
4. When on a forty-day fast, the wilderness (hardship) seals God's commands in our hearts and minds.
5. When on a forty-day fast, we are preparing for victory over our greatest enemies.

My hope for those of you who never have entered into a forty-day fast is that when you read this chapter, you will see the important role of a forty-day fast in the development of your life, ministry, business, and such. And I pray that you will be stirred by the Holy Spirit to enter into one with His help and guidance.

This chapter deals specifically with the forty-day fast. Going on a fast that involves abstaining from food and water for forty days and nights must be supported by divine guidance and heavenly intervention. It will take a supernatural move of the Spirit of God to enable you to physically survive without water for such a long period of time. For this reason, I urge you not to enter into a forty-day fast in which you abstain from water for forty days and nights unless you are certain that the power of the Spirit of God is upon you to do so. Instead, you may consider fasting for forty days but not nights, which is from 6:00 a.m. to 6:00 p.m. to represent the days, abstaining from food and water. Or you may fast for forty days and nights, abstaining from food only but drinking lots of water. Both of these methods of fasting must also not be entered into lightly, for all forty-day fasts must be spirit-led and empowered by the Holy Spirit. Remember, God only approves of deeds that come from a heart that is set on pleasing Him and not as a display of your own righteousness or willpower. For deeds that please Him, reflect genuine love; that is, the willingness to be used by God and to stand in the gap for others.

Key 1—Abide in the Mountain of God

"When I was gone up into the mountain to receive the tables of stones, even the tables of the covenant which the Lord made with you, then I abode in the mountain forty days and forty nights, I neither did eat bread not drink water" (Deuteronomy 9:9).

Mountains—A Place of Governance

Whenever embarking on the forty-day fast, we ought to "go up" onto the mountain to meet with God. Mountains are symbolic of governmental systems because they are masses of land that tower high above the plains. When on a mountain, it grants us a clearer overall perspective of the land below it. Mountains are visible to all who are on the plains below, making them a great landmark or point of reference. To get to the top of the mountain, however, requires great effort. Mountains are locations on earth that place you closer to heaven. When God made man, He made him from the dust of the earth. The dust that is closest to heaven can be found on mountaintops. By this I mean that there is a place called the mountain, where humans (who are made from the dust of the earth) can abide and be nearer to heaven.

But what does the scripture mean in reference to the mountain? It refers to a place of governance or ruling. Isaiah spoke about mountains in this way: "It shall come to pass in the last days that the Mountain of the LORD's house shall be established in the top of the mountains" (Isaiah 2:2–4 KJV). The Mountain of the Lord's house speaks of the governmental system of God's kingdom, by which the kingdoms of this world will be governed. Daniel became a witness to this prophecy through the revelation of a dream that Nebuchadnezzar, the king of Babylon, had. In this dream, the Lord revealed to Daniel that the kingdom of God was going to rest upon and rule over all the kingdoms of the earth. This heavenly government would be reestablished in the earth "in the last days," which we are currently in.

This Mountain Is in Us

When God made humankind, He created them in His image. The scriptures state, "So God created mankind in his own image, in the image of God he created them; male and female he created them" (Genesis 1:27). God intended to make humankind in His image and likeness, and this work was expressed in this way: "Then the LORD God formed a man from the dust of the ground and breathed into his nostrils the breath of life, and the man became a living being" (Genesis 2:7). To form means to make from something. This means that God took something to form the man; He took the man He created and the dust of the ground to form him in His image and likeness. Though the image of the man was like God, who is Spirit, the likeness of God in the man was a work in progress. To establish godlikeness in the man, God had to establish His word within the man. It is God's commands that ought to govern everyone, making the Word of God the law that established the government of God in us. When God's law has preeminence in us, it rules over the way we live. God's law becomes like a mountain that towers above every other way of life.

The prophet Isaiah had this to say about the government of God: "For to us a child is born, to us a son is given, and *the government will be on his shoulders ...*" (Isaiah 9:6, emphasis added). The child spoken of in this scripture is Jesus. He bears the responsibility of establishing God's government. And Jesus continually spoke of the need for people to believe in Him so that He might abide in them and them in Him. When He abides in us, He establishes God's government in us. This is why I said the mountain is in us. So when Moses spoke of going up onto the mountain to meet with God during his forty-day fast, the mountain refers to a place within our souls where God establishes His government. To go up the mountain means allowing the Word of God to gain more precedence in our hearts. To go up the mountain means pursuing another level of understanding in the Word of God. It also means a willingness to change our perspective on the way we once saw life, to live by higher standards. It is in the soul that the believers in Jesus who fast can expect to encounter the governing rule of God, where God establishes His will, and where our wills are diminished. This is a place of submission to God, where His desires are transferred to us, to see His kingdom and government expanded to the lives of others, where we see things from His perspective.

Mountains are usually steep, and to climb one requires perseverance. The higher the mountain the greater the perseverance that is required to climb it. The perseverance I am speaking of is persistence in prayer, and in reading and meditating on the Scriptures. Through prayer, and reading and meditating on the scripture, we ascend to a meeting place with God within our souls. Ascending to a meeting place with God coupled with the sacrifice of fasting is like bringing a love sacrifice up the mountain unto God. This reminds me of Abraham who brought his only son Isaac to the mountain God specified so that he may offer him there as a sacrifice. It was in that setting that God said He now knew that Abraham loved Him. You see, fasting with prayer and meditating on the scripture lets God know that you truly love Him. To do so is to come to Him with the greatest love gift you could ever offer, which is expressed in fasting.

Encountering God on the Mountains

When we go up the mountain, we'll encounter three main platforms from which God governs:

- the temple of the Lord
- the courts of heaven
- the throne of God

For each place, God rules as God over all, judge over all, and King over all. As God over all, God desires to reside in us as His temple. As judge over all, God is responsible for pronouncing judgment in the fullness of time upon everyone, in direct response to their deeds. And as King over all, God has dominion and rule over all, and all things are subject to Him.

In this chapter I'd like to emphasize God's role as the ruler in our temples. God created each of us like a three-part temple, where the innermost chamber is called the spirit. This chamber is where the Holy Spirit is meant to dwell, and God speaks from that place. When God made Adam, He first filled this spirit chamber with His breath, which was a symbol of the vocal presence of God, or God's voice, through the presence of the Holy Spirit. The scripture tells us that the breath was placed through Adam's nostrils, not through his mouth. The nostrils are the part of our bodies that do not depend on sight but on discernment and knowing. Like nostrils, the spirit of man functions in us mainly through discerning and knowing. In Adam, the breath of God that was placed in his spirit connected his soul to God. This connection did not make Adam alive but connected him to life in God and purpose, turning his soul that was already alive into a living soul.

The soul is like the middle chamber, where the Word is meant to dwell. The purpose and guidance that came from within the spirit of the man was meant to give meaning to the Word residing in the soul. In other words, the soul finds its purpose from the connection that exists with the one who resides in the spirit. But when sin was introduced into the equation, the breath was taken away, and there was a disconnection between the man's spirit and the breath that resided in his spirit. This disconnection made the man spiritually dead, and, in a sense, his soul died because it no longer had the connection that established purpose and provided guidance from God. A living soul finds purpose and life from God, but a dead soul is disconnected from this purpose and life. It exists only for itself, without a government or ruler.

This is how sin made humankind available and open to have the devil establish his governmental (worldly) system in them. This is where God's work to restore and reestablish a heavenly governmental system within us comes in. God desires to restore our souls and make them "live" again. But to be effective, the middle chamber, which is the soul, must once again be filled with the Word that the Spirit uses to guide and give purpose to the soul. This is why God seeks people who are willing to come up to a place where He can give them the necessary words for the restoration of their souls.

I like to use the example of a smartphone in describing this restoration. The hard drive within the phone, which gives it the ability to make and take calls, is like the "soul" of the phone—this ability directly relates to the device's purpose. The spirit of the phone would be like the SIM (subscriber identity module) card that allows the phone to communicate with the service provider, which is what gives the phone true character in relation to its purpose. When the phone is powered up and has a hard drive and a SIM card, but it's not connected to a service provider, all you can do is play games or take pictures. The phone can't perform its fundamental function—to make calls.

Like a smart phone, the purpose of our lives comes from the connection we have with our "service provider"—God. Only when we are connected to God and there is continual communication between Him and us can we truly perform our fundamental function. That function is not playing games but being useful to our Owner, with the ability to do what we were created to do, which is to please God.

The initiating of a restorative work regarding the purpose of individuals can come about through a forty-day fast. For this reason it is necessary to go up onto the mountain and abide there until we receive a command (word) from God. When we fast like this, we are joining in purpose with God by becoming a vessel through which God can bring the restoration of His heavenly system within the souls of individuals. This is why Moses fasted for forty days and nights, so that he could receive what would bring restoration to the people of Israel. Remember, the people did not receive the full commandments when they heard God speak the Ten Commandments from heaven, so God told Moses to come up into the mountain so that he could receive the full commandments in fasting for forty days and nights.

Key 2—The Tables of the Covenant

"At the end of the forty days and forty nights, the LORD gave me the two stone tablets, the tablets of the covenant" (Deuteronomy 9:11).

In the King James Version of the Bible, the above scripture is, "The Lord gave me the tables of stone, even the tables of the covenant." The *table of stone* and the *table of the covenant* refer to two aspects of the same thing. The table of stone was the written version of the Ten Commandments that God spoke from the mountain out of heaven to the nation of Israel. The scripture records Moses as saying, "The LORD gave me two stone tablets inscribed by the finger of God. On them were all the commandment the LORD proclaimed to you on the mountain out of the fire, on the day of the assembly" (Deuteronomy 9:10). Yet the Ten Commandments were not the full commandments in the sense that they did not explain God's heart concerning His commands. His heart was hidden within those commands, and He desired that the people seek to know it. In knowing God's heart, they would know who He truly is. When God called Moses up on the mountain into a forty-day fast, He gave him the full commandments in the form of ordinances.

These ordinances were the terms of a covenant that God wanted to establish with His people. When God sent Moses back to the people, He sent him with two things that would represent what God wanted to do later on in the hearts of His people. The table of stones represents our hearts, upon which God desires to write His laws and commands. The same table of stone was called the table of the covenant, for God wants to establish a covenant with us through the commands He gives. The significance of why God gave the tablet of stone to Moses on the mountain was expressed by Jeremiah when he wrote, "This is the covenant I will make with the people of Israel after that time, declares The Lord. I will put my law in their minds and write it on their hearts. I will be their God and they will be my people" (Jeremiah 31:33). This scripture in the book of Jeremiah, though written thousands of years ago, speaks of what we experience today in our lives.

God has brought His Word to us in the manifestation of Jesus Christ and has etched in our hearts a love for Him and for others.

Moses gave the people the full commandments, which began this way: "Hear, O Israel: The LORD our God, the LORD is one. Love the LORD your God with all your heart and with all your soul and with all your strength" (Deuteronomy 6:4–5). When Jesus was asked what the greatest commandment was, He repeated this scripture and included another, saying, "And the second is like it: 'Love your neighbor as yourself.' All the Law and the Prophets hang on these two commandments" (Matthew 22:35).

Because the laws or commandments are hinged around this commandment of love, if we live by the love that is etched in our hearts when we became children of God, then we will manifest the heavenly system God ordained to be on the earth. The scripture also speaks of a transition from the old system to the new; that is, from living "in the shadow of the thing" to living in the thing itself. As God promised through Ezekiel, "I will give you a new heart and put a new spirit in you; I will remove from you your heart of stone and give you a heart of flesh" (Ezekiel 36:26). This speaks of the passing away of the method by which God communicated His commands and sent word for restoration; that is, the writing of laws on a table of stone and a table of the covenant. But now God has made it the way it should be by placing His Word in our hearts and minds. In doing so, He makes a covenant with us to be our God.

The prophet also refers to "a heart of flesh." A heart of flesh represents the heart people ought to have. God created humans with hearts made of flesh, not made of stone. The etching of laws on stone was a representation of the burning of God's Word in the hearts of men. This is what we can expect to receive when we go up the mountain to receive from God. Moses also said that "the words were written on the stone by the finger of God." Jesus once described His miracles by saying that the people were seeing the "finger of God." We know that the Spirit of the Lord was upon Jesus, who anointed Him to do miracles. This means that the finger of God is the work of the Holy Spirit. He is the one who etches the words in our hearts and gives understanding to our minds.

Previously I mentioned that the mountain represents the Word of God within our souls, and climbing the mountain refers to the ascent into God's

Word to see from God's perspective. I also mentioned that the Spirit within our spirits gives meaning to the Word of God we receive in our souls. This Spirit is referred to in the passage of scripture that states, "The LORD gave me two stone tablets inscribed by the *finger of God*" (Deuteronomy 9:10, emphasis added). So when the scripture states that while on the mountain, Moses received the two stone tablets inscribed by the finger of God, this speaks of the work of the Holy Spirit embedding the commands of God in our hearts while we spend time in His Word during a fast. The Holy Spirit not only gives higher understanding of the Word of God, but He also gives the power to keep the terms of the what we came to understand. This is represented by the table of the covenant.

The covenant is the means through which God causes us to inherit what He promised to give us. For this reason, God desires to etch the willingness to keep the terms of the covenant in our hearts by the power of the Holy Spirit. This guarantees that we come into possession of the promises of God.

During a forty-day fast, if we abide on the mountain, then we are in a place where we can commune with God concerning His vision for others. God expresses His vision through His commandments, which is first given to those who are eligible to access the vision in the presence of God. God did this with Moses in the wilderness, for the scripture states, "And He said unto Moses, Come up unto the Lord, thou, and Aaron, Nadab, and Abihu, and seventy of the elders of Israel; and worship ye afar off. And Moses alone shall come near the Lord: but they shall not come nigh; neither shall the people go up with him" (Exodus 24:1–2). Not everyone was willing to lay down their lives as Moses was. The people rejected God's method of communication because they saw death for themselves, but Moses saw an opportunity to meet with God, though it may involve death. The scripture speaks about Moses's response to the terrifying acts of God on Mount Sinai in this way:

"You have not come to a mountain that can be touched and that is burning with fire; to darkness, gloom and storm; to a trumpet blast or to such a voice speaking words that those (referring to the Israelites who were in the wilderness) who heard it begged that no further word be spoken to them, because they could not bear what was commanded: 'If even an animal touches the mountain, it must be stoned to death'. The sight was so terrifying that Moses said, 'I am trembling with fear'" (Hebrews 12:18–21 KJV). And though Moses was trembling and afraid, he did not allow that to stop him from entering into that thick darkness while the people stood far off. The scriptures recorded: "The people remained at a distance, while Moses approached the thick darkness where God was" (Exodus 20:21).

The scripture also tells us why Moses alone was to come up on the mountain. When God spoke the Ten Commandments to the people, audibly from the mountain, they were afraid of the manner in which God communicated with them and asked for a mediator. God approved of this and called Moses to come up on the mountain to receive the full commandments. It is in the full commandments that we can better see the heart of God and not merely His rules, which is how many of the people saw the Ten Commandments. This willingness to enter into the unknown, a place of terrifying commands in the face of death, in order to access God made Moses eligible to receive commands and vision that express God's heart on behalf of the people and for the people.

Though God gave the vision to Moses, it was ultimately for all of Israel, just as God gave the commandments to Israel, but it was ultimately for the whole world. It was given to Israel so they might use the commands of God to impact and influence the world as a nation of priests. Moses gave record and said, "Now therefore, if ye will obey my voice indeed, and keep my covenant, then ye shall be a peculiar treasure unto me above all people: for all the earth is mine: And ye shall be unto me a kingdom of priests, and an holy nation. These are the words which thou shalt speak unto the children of Israel" (Exodus 19:5–6 KJV). This says to us today that if we approach God with a willingness to lay down our lives in a forty-day fast, though we may be afraid of the consequences to ourselves because of the fast, we will enter a place where God gives us a part of His vision for the world. It is through this vision that God will establish His mountain on the tops of the mountain; it is through such visions that Jesus our Lord will establish a heavenly government that rests upon His shoulders. That is the strength of the Word of God. This vision would enable the people of God to impact and influence the people around them for the glory of God.

God Gives Us Words of Restoration on the Mountains

When God led the people of Israel through the wilderness, He caused them to "fast," in a sense, for forty years (which was supposed to be for forty days and nights). He did this to equip them to be used to bring the power of restoration to the world. The scriptures describe Israel's fast this way: "Remember how the LORD your God led you all the way in the wilderness these forty years, to humble and test you in order to know what was in your heart, whether or not you would keep his commands. He humbled you, causing you to hunger and then feeding you with manna, which neither you nor your ancestors had known, to teach you that man does not live on bread alone but on every word that comes from the mouth of the LORD" (Deuteronomy 8:2–3). God made the people of Israel fast and gave them a symbol of the revelation that would come down from heaven. This manna, which was called "what," speaks of the revelation of God of which individuals were meant to partake. Preceding this revelation was a hunger for God, thus making manna God's response to their hunger. The revelation of God's Word is God's response to those who go on a forty-day fast. Remember, the stone was cut and prepared by God; then Moses was used to reveal the commands of God. In the same way, fasting involves the preparing a heart and pressing into God's Word. This results in the etching of the commands, which is revelation of God's Word.

God Gives Us the Plans and Strategies for Restoration on the Mountains

Earlier I spoke about the vision that God gives to us when we come up the mountain in fasting. It isn't coincidental that our vision is far better when we are on a mountaintop. Vision is God's main objective for us when we enter a forty-day fast. In order to carry out a successful mission, there must be a vision, then a plan, then a strategy, and finally the execution of the strategy. When on a forty-day fast, God not only gives us a vision but a plan and a strategy as well. Like Moses, Elijah also fasted for forty days and nights, and God gave him a plan for the removal of Baal from the land. Before Elijah received the plan, he misunderstood God's approach to restoring Israel. But after he went on a forty-day fast, the plan and strategy was revealed to him. Unfortunately, Elijah did not come up the mountain with a heart that was prepared. When he got up the mountain with a heart that wanted to give up, he received the revelation of God, but it was not etched in his heart. This is why he did not carry out the plan as it was given to him. We too must be careful, lest we enter into a forty-day fast with the wrong heart, and though we receive the plan and strategy of God, we still fail to carry it out in a way that pleases Him.

Finally, Jesus also fasted for forty days and nights in the wilderness, so that He could set in motion the restoration of all people. After His forty-day fast, the scriptures state that He hungered. This hunger is the usual result of a forty-day fast. I'm not referring to a physical hunger; rather, it was a hunger for God's vision, plan, and strategy. Jesus hungered for the revelation of God. A heart that is prepared to receive from God will receive, just as the scriptures state: "Blessed are those who hunger and thirst for righteousness, for they will be filled" (Matthew 5:6). And now we know what can lead to a hunger for righteousness.

All of these forty-day fasts were for the initiating of a restoration that God wanted to bring about in the hearts of people other than themselves. In so doing, God used these men to establish His governmental system within many hearts. We should also be willing to be used by God in fasting this way, so that we too will do our parts to bring about this restoration of the kingdom of God within the souls of others. This commission to work and establish God's governmental system happens when we abide on the mountain of God.

As I mentioned at the start of this book, God revealed to me the things I've written in this book while I was on a forty-day fast. Unbeknownst to me at the time, I was receiving expressions of God's heart concerning fasting, to be expressed as commands from the Lord in this book. I pray this becomes a challenge for you, as the Spirit compels you to see the cause for a forty-day fast. For now, you know better than I did when I entered into such a fast, yet I received from God wonderful words of life. How much more would you be likely to knowingly and with expectation (which is faith) receive a life-changing word?

Key 3—Entering by the Leading of the Holy Spirit

"Moses entered the cloud and went up on the mountain. And Moses was on the mountain forty days and forty nights" (Exodus 24:18 ESV).

Did you notice that the scripture says, "Moses entered the cloud *and* went up on the mountain." For it to happen in this way, Moses had to have first entered the cloud, and then he went up on the mountain. This order seems contrary to what we might expect. Usually, we'd expect it to say, "Moses went up the mountain and entered into the cloud," since clouds are typically seen high up the mountain. But God, in His wisdom, arranged for Moses to enter the cloud before going up on the mountain. He did it to symbolize the protocol in which we engage when we enter into a forty-day fast.

Entering the cloud speaks of encountering God's glory before we can receive the revelation of God on the mountain. In other words, God engages us to enter into a forty-day fast. I believe that this is the case for all types of fasts. But I also believe there is a special encounter worth mentioning when entering a forty-day fast. For me, it started with the special move of the Spirit when He caused the book *Fasting That Moves God's Hand* by T. L. Lowery to supernaturally come to the church door. And when He led me to receive the book *Fasting* by Jentezen Franklin as a gift, He used it to invite me into my first forty-day fast. It may be different for you, but however He calls you, do not be afraid, as the people were, refusing to submit to the Holy Spirit.

When the people saw the cloud come down the mountain, it was terrifying to them; it was terrifying to Moses as well. But the difference between the people and Moses is that Moses did not succumb to his fear, and he submitted to the call of God. The scripture states: "The people remained at a distance, while Moses approached the thick darkness where God was" (Exodus 20:21). And Moses did not presume to enter the cloud of his own accord, for it was the Lord who summoned him. This means that entering the cloud speaks of submission to the call of the Spirit of God.

Moses's entering the cloud and going up on the mountain, where he fasted, represents being led by the Holy Spirit into a forty-day fast. The cloud was one of the physical manifestations of the glorious presence of God. This glorious manifestation today is experienced through the presence of the Holy Spirit. So when we fast, we must seek to be guided by the Holy Spirit into the presence of God. It is by the Holy Spirit that we get into the place of governance, where God awaits to give us the instruction that He wants us to teach others. Moses received the commandments upon tables of stones but by the power of the Holy Spirit. Today we receive the commandments of God written on the tables of our hearts and minds. Only the Holy Spirit can bring about the restorative end that God desires after a forty-day fast, so entering into one must not be by our own presumption but by instruction. If the Holy Spirit is not with us on such a venture, there will be no dynamic power available to carry out the work necessary for manifesting fruitfulness.

Let's look at some of the works of the Holy Spirit in relation to restoration and fruitfulness to see how expedient He is in the process. The scriptures state that in the beginning, God created the heavens and the earth. But when the earth was described in the second verse of Genesis 1, it was in a state of emptiness and chaos, which resulted in the fruitlessness of the earth. I believe God created the earth this way to reflect the unfruitful state of the earth and the dust of the ground that is absent of His presence and purpose. But I won't expound on that matter here. Just imagine all the creatures and plants that would require order to live when being made while the earth was in a chaotic state. They also would have been as useless as the chaotic earth they would have inhabited. The scripture goes on to say that "the Spirit of a God hovered over the face of the deep." It was after the Spirit came upon the earth that there was a power to bring about restoration by the commands of God. This is the work of the Holy Spirit—to precede the commands of God, making the place of His presence conducive for God's commands to take effect.

When the people of Israel were leaving Egypt, the scriptures states, they were led by a pillar of cloud by day and a pillar of fire by night. These pillars eventually led them to the Red Sea, which, when they crossed over, brought them to the wilderness, where they were to fast for forty days. At a glance, the purpose of the two pillars would appear to be a cloud for needed shade in the daytime and fire for needed light at night. But there is more significance to what God was doing when He manifested the cloud and the fire. The cloud would have prevented the people of Israel from seeing any other way of deliverance than following the cloud.

In the same way, we are to be guided by the Holy Spirit and should not seek other means of getting to God's planned destination for our lives. It is God's holy cloud, the Holy Spirit, who must lead us into the wilderness. This brings me to Jesus, our Lord, who was led by the Spirit into the wilderness, where He fasted for forty days and nights. Though Jesus was and is the Son of God, He did not enter into that fast except by the leading of the Holy Spirit. Unlike the people of Israel in their wilderness, Jesus acknowledged that God, who led Him into the wilderness, was able to keep Him and sustain Him while He was in the wilderness. It is God who sustains us when we enter into a forty-day fast.

The sustenance, in this case, is not merely our physical bodies but our souls. The purpose of the wilderness was to tempt, test, and prove the character of the one who was led into it. But praise God that we find, within the wilderness, the mountain of God and His commands and covenant. Only the Spirit can navigate us through the testing, temptations, and hardships to a place in ourselves where we can receive a word from God that will change our hearts and then impact and influence the lives many others.

In these last days, God has revealed more and more about His glory to His children. The result is that people are making more room for God to stretch out His hand to work in the midst of His people. In such glory, many are healed and delivered, with great signs and wonders. There are various levels of glory, which refers to the various dimensions in which God moves. I believe that when we enter into a forty-day fast we enter into one of these dimensions where God stretches out His hands to heal, deliver, and save. I say this because of the amazing things the scriptures recorded as the aftermath of a forty-day fast.

Key 4—The Wilderness Seals God's Commands in Our Minds

> "Then Jesus was led up by the Spirit into the wilderness
> to be tempted by the devil. And after fasting forty days
> and forty nights, He was hungry" (Matthew 4:1–2 ESV).

Part of every believer's journey in the Christian life is the wilderness experiences, for this is where sanctification for his or her true purpose and preparation for inheriting God's promises occurs. Two purposes are pursued in the wilderness: God's purpose and the accuser's (Satan's) purpose. God's intents are to use the hardships we face in the wilderness to strengthen and perfect us; to make us ready for greater usefulness for Him. The accuser's purpose in the wilderness is to attempt to show us and God that we are not fit or capable of being used by God to restore the earth to be under a heavenly government. It's true that we cannot be fruitful in accomplishing our created purpose of manifesting the kingdom of God by our own strength and wisdom. "For the Kingdom of God is not a matter of what we eat or drink, but of living a life of goodness and peace and joy in the Holy Spirit" (Romans 14:17 NLT).

This means that the only way we can manifest the kingdom of a God is by the presence and power of the Holy Spirit. This is why the Spirit of God is with us in the wilderness, to guide us in the midst of the accuser's temptations. The scripture states: "So shall they fear the name of the LORD from the west, and His glory from the rising of the sun. When the enemy shall come in like a flood, the Spirit of the LORD shall lift up a standard against him" (Isaiah 59:19 KJV). I like the King James Version of this scripture because of the way it speaks of the Lord's lifting up a "standard" that works against the enemy. Another version phrase it this way: "For he [that is, the enemy] will come like a rushing stream, which the wind of the LORD drives" (Isaiah 59:19 ESV). This says that though the accuser is planning an onslaught of temptations, the standard or measure of the onslaught will be regulated by the Holy Spirit.

The scripture also states: "No temptation has overtaken you except what is common to mankind. And God is faithful; He will not let you be tempted beyond what you can bear. But when you are tempted, He will also provide a way out so that you can endure it" (1 Corinthians 10:13 ESV). This means that God, who governs all, determines the limits of your test, and the tempter cannot go beyond it, or it will no longer be an appropriate test for you. Not only does God set limits for the test, but He gives grace, for the scripture again states: "Let us then approach God's throne of grace with confidence, so that we may receive mercy and find grace to help us in our time of need" (Hebrews 4:16 NLT).

In God's presence we find grace to help us when we need it most. What better place to depend upon God's grace than the wilderness, a place of testing and temptations. This grace is not to remove us from the wilderness but to help. This is the work of the Holy Spirit, which is to help, for He is our helper.

When we are in the wilderness, we are tested to reveal the true states of our hearts. When the Word of God is not in our hearts, nor are His commands clear in our minds, we cannot prove the preeminence of the kingdom of God. But God, in His wisdom, uses the wilderness to scorch His Word in our hearts and minds, using the wilderness as a form of fiery trials. The scripture also speaks of how we ought to see these fiery trials, saying, "Dear friends, don't be surprised at the fiery trials you are going through, as if something strange were happening to you" (1 Peter 4:12 NLT).

We should not be surprised because the purpose of the trials is to perfect us. The book of James states, "For you know that when your faith is tested, your endurance has a chance to grow" (James 1:3 NLT). This is God's wisdom in the trials we face in the wilderness, which we enter into even during or after a forty-day fast. Because we know the purpose of the wilderness and its fiery trials, we should be glad about what we will face, as the book of James also states, "Consider it all joy, my brethren, when you encounter various trials" (James 1:2 NASB). When God gives us the commandments written in our hearts and minds, the trials we face ought to help us grow into them. The fruit we display in the midst of the fiery trials of the wilderness proves our hearts to be true unto God.

If we do not bear fruit, it testifies that God's commands did not penetrate our hearts. Jesus spoke about this when He told the parable of the sower and the seed. Jesus told of the seeds that fell on stony ground. The seeds grew up quickly, but the sun, which should have helped them, destroyed them. Jesus later revealed the meaning of the parable by saying that it spoke of a type of heart that does not allow the word that is heard to get deep in the soul because of the stony (stubborn) nature of the heart. If we possess stubborn minds, this can prevent the commands God gives us in the time of fasting from getting into a place of transformation. Then, God can only destroy those stubborn characteristics by repetitious circling around the mountain, where God patiently and strategically removes that kind of thinking.

The inheritance we ought to possess will be on hold for a much longer time because of a stubborn heart. As it was with the Israelites, whatever believing brings in a day, stubbornness can turn into a year's journey. When I mention inheritance, I mean the promise of God for our lives, which He gave to Abraham when He said, "Through you shall all the families of the earth be blessed." This is our inheritance, to be a conduit for blessing the world around us. But this takes character that can be formed only in the wilderness. And if we hold on to stubborn, rebellious attitudes toward God's command, we put the blessing of our families, friends, and many who are around us on hold.

During Jesus's fast, He received God's instructions concerning His ministry, but before He entered into His ministry, He was led by the Spirit of God into the wilderness of testing. Did Jesus truly relinquish His privileges as the Son of God? Did He really submit to the Father's agenda for Him, now that He was a man? Would Jesus sin, just as Adam had sinned in the garden? These are some of the questions that were answered when Jesus was tested in the wilderness. Because He did not yield to the temptations in the wilderness, it validates that He possessed the character to carry out God's redemptive plan. So when Jesus was tempted to turn the stone to bread, He did not take up the privileges. He laid them down. Had He taken up His privileges, He would have placed His needs before others and wouldn't have been the servant He was sent to be.

If the tempter came against the Son of God, then how much more will he think he can succeed against us? For us to have victory, we must do what Jesus did to have victory over the tempter—He used God's commands. Jesus used the lessons learned from the Israelite's experiences in the wilderness to gain His victory in the wilderness. He knew that the real test was not from an external tempter but within His own heart.

Jesus did not harden His heart to God's Word, nor did He refuse to trust God when placed under pressure in His wilderness. Instead, Jesus submitted Himself to God through trusting in the Father's instructions and resisting the accuser. Jesus fasted forty days and nights before entering His work for the Father, The wilderness sealed the Father's commands in Jesus's heart and mind. We must be prepared to do as Jesus did in the wilderness we experience so we will have the same success.

Key Number 5—Preparation for Victory over Our Greatest Enemy

"And the tempter came and said to Him, If You are the Son of God, command these stones to become loaves of bread. But He answered, It is written, Man shall not live by bread alone, but by every word that comes from the mouth of God" (Matthew 4:3–4 ESV).

Man shall not live by bread alone but by every word that comes from the mouth of God. This is the outcome that God is working within the hearts of those who enter into a forty-day fast. God seeks a resolve within our hearts that indicates that we are ready to enter into the Promised Land. When the accuser tempted Jesus to eat in the wilderness, Jesus answered the tempter with the words Moses proclaimed to the people of Israel when they were in their wilderness.

> Remember how the LORD your God led you through the wilderness for these forty years, humbling you and testing you to prove your character, and to find out whether or not you would obey his commands. Yes, He humbled you by letting you go hungry and then feeding you with manna, a food previously unknown to you and your ancestors. He did it to teach you that people do not live by bread alone; rather, we live by every word that comes from the mouth of the LORD. For all these forty years your clothes didn't wear out, and your feet didn't blister or swell. Think about it:Just as a parent disciplines a child, the LORD your God disciplines you for your own good. (Deuteronomy 8:2–5 NLT)

Fasting and the wilderness experience were disciplinary strategies that God used to teach the people to put their total trust in His commands, rather than their personal yearnings or feelings. It was through the process of fasting and the wilderness experience that Israel overcame their greatest enemy and obstacles. Their greatest enemy and obstacles were not the tempter or the giants, as the Israelites once thought, or the walls of Jericho. Instead, Israel's greatest enemy was the ungodly character within their own hearts. Ungodly character has been the greatest enemy humankind has encountered, and every person has faced that enemy. That enemy is the true enemy of the soul, literally working against the soul for its demise. Fear, spiritual blindness, lust, disobedience, contentiousness—these are only some of the ungodly characteristics that lie within us, preventing us from inheriting the character of the "promised man."

Think about it; it is ungodly character that causes the soul to be cast into hell. Character reflects the nature or inherent qualities of something or someone. If the inherent quality of something is flawed, then its own character will lead to its destruction. For example, say you owned a factory that manufactured tires, and a batch of the tires you made all had an inherent flaw that could cause them to deflate under normal pressure. If these tires were sold to the general public, they would cause more harm than good, not only to the tires but to the car and everyone in it. Because the problem with the tires is an inherent one, the characteristics of the tires are what need to be repaired. To repair inherent problems in a tire takes more than just a patch; it takes breaking down the tire for reconstruction. This is the only way the tire can work without putting the car and driver in jeopardy.

This is the wisdom God used with Israel in the wilderness. He placed them in a situation that broke people down to show their true colors, and then He reconstructed them with His Word. The results were brand-new people who had the right character to inherit what God promised them.

What a blessed result that came from the discipline of God—a renewed character made ready to walk in the calling of God; possessing the Promised Land while in the wilderness of discipline; becoming the person God promised to make of Abraham and his descendants. God promised to change us into a conduit of blessing to the families of the earth. The Promised Land that He wants to show us is a "promised man" that He is opening our eyes to become; that is, a person whose life produces milk, which is needed for nutrients, and honey, needed for sweetness and adding flavor.

My prayer is that you desire to become that person of godly character, who is made ready to be a blessing on the earth, just as God originally intended. God said, "Be fruitful, multiply fruitfulness, fill the earth by multiplying fruitfulness, and manage or maintain the fruitfulness that was multiplied and has filled the earth."

This mandate that God gave us was not merely about having children or building houses but about filling the earth with the goodness of God. Do not be suborned, as the people of Israel were, and delay your own inheritance, for the delay only reduces the time of fruitfulness, which leads to regret. Yet as God, in His mercy, sent them back to the process and was patient, waiting as long as it took to remove the stubbornness from the people's hearts, so also I pray that God will be merciful to His stubborn children. If you have been stubborn about submitting to God's call for your life, stop your stubbornness, and submit to God. If you have yielded to every temptation that the devil presents to you to please yourself, seek God's correction, and submit to His discipline. God is merciful and will go great lengths to restore you, but you must seek mercy. The heart that seeks mercy shows a readiness for restoration, and anything that is not restored is destroyed. If you do not cry out for mercy, then you are still stiff-necked and heading for danger. Mercy is for an appointed time, and after that comes judgment.

CHAPTER 5

Preparing Your Land for Fruitfulness

Then I will hear from heaven, and I will forgive
their sin and will heal their land.
—2 Chronicles 7:14

To understand the scripture above, we must understand what is meant by "the land." In the Old Testament many nations are named by their geographic locations. People who lived on the hillsides were called hill-dwellers. People who lived in the plains were called plain-dwellers. Because a nation of people lived in the valleys, they were called people of the lowlands. Some may assume that the people of that time were called by their location for easy identification. While that may be true, God had a greater reason for naming people based on where they lived. Places like the lands of Egypt, Canaan, or the lands of the Amorites, Hittites, and such referred to the character of the people who dwelled there. God used the method of identifying one's character by associating them with the land where they lived. He did this to help us perceive the character He wants to displace from and to add to our lives.

The Land

Genesis 12 records that God told Abram the land of Canaan was the Promised Land. The Canaanites were people of the lowland, or plains; this signified a low, debased, carnal, or fleshly character. But God wanted those who would believe Him to possess—that is, to rule over—the fleshly character. Though Canaan represented the fleshly nature, God promised Abram that the place where the fleshly nature once ruled would become a place of blessing. For the people of Israel to eventually possess Canaan, they had to dispossess the Canaanites who lived there. This speaks of displacing the fleshly nature from ruling in our bodies, so that while we are in the body we can please God. The apostle Paul wrote, "Therefore do not let sin reign in your mortal body so that you obey its evil desires" (Romans 6:13). This required the transformation that God desires to work in everyone who heeds His call—to separate themselves from this world. In essence, God desires to transform our fleshly lives into lives from which He will pour out His spiritual blessings. This is why God, speaking of things that were not as they were, called the land of Canaan a land flowing with milk and honey. In doing this, He guaranteed that those who would obey Him would be transformed from carnal people to children of promise.

It seems that God wants to heal the land so that it can be fruitful. This reminds me that when God created the earth (which is natural), it was without form and void. At that time the earth was not yet filled with heaven (which is spiritual). The earth in this state was unfruitful and without usefulness. It was as if the earth needed to be healed. But when God put His Word of light into the earth, it dispossessed the darkness. This was the first step to making the earth ready to be fruitful. This goes to show that from the very beginning, God demonstrated His eagerness to make humans (the dust of the ground) fruitful.

Just as God created the heavens and the earth, God created humankind. The book of Genesis states, "So God created mankind in his own image, in the image of God he created them; male and female he created them" (Genesis 1:27). The scripture tells us that God is Spirit. This is the image of God. He is not like Spirit, but He is Spirit. Humankind was created spirit in the image of God and was placed within the earthly form that God made from the dust of the ground, so that the dust would be more than just dust.

The book of Genesis also records, "Then the Lord God formed a man from the dust of the ground and breathed into his nostrils the breath of life, and the man became a living being" (Genesis 2:7). The man formed from the dust of the earth was natural, just as the earth is natural. Without God's Word and breath, the natural man would also be without form and void. The natural or carnal man without God is described as the flesh. But when God spoke words of dominion into the man formed from the dust and breathed into him, it was like heaven entering earth. It was after this moment that man formed of flesh became a fruitful man.

Cultivating the Land

"Now no shrub had yet appeared on the earth and no plant had yet sprung up, for the Lord God had not sent rain on the earth and there was no one to work the ground" (Genesis 2:5).

As I pondered more on the land, I thought about the work that God intended for man to do with the land. The book of Genesis tells us the Lord would not pour rain on the earth because there was no man to cultivate the ground. The rain is symbolic of the grace of God for growth, and the ground or land is symbolic of our bodies that must be cultivated for fruitfulness. To cultivate the land is to make it ready for planting. Before God planted the trees of the earth, He was waiting for a man—that is, a cultivated body. As the scriptures record, "Therefore, when Christ came into the world, he said: "Sacrifice and offering you did not desire, but a body you prepared for me" (Hebrews 10:5). The body that is prepared by God speaks of a person who is made ready (cultivated) to be used by God to manifest fruitfulness in the lives of others. Cultivation of the land speaks of a dispossession of things that make the land unfruitful. Remember that although the earth in itself is unfruitful, with heaven's intervention the earth is blessed to be a blessing.

We see an example of grace given to humankind through a body in the life of Noah. In his day the people of the earth were wicked and unfruitful. So God pronounced judgment over the entire world because of the unfruitfulness of humankind. Remember that God's judgments are good, and even in this judgment God was going to work out righteousness. In order to pour out rain upon the earth, God would prepare Noah to become a body that was cultivated to produce a fruitful end. As the scripture states, "So the Lord said, "I will wipe from the face of the earth the human race I have created—and with them the animals, the birds and the creatures that move along the ground—for I regret that I have made them." But Noah found favor in the eyes of the Lord" (Genesis 6:7–8).

Other translations of this scripture use the word *grace* in place of *favor*. So Noah found grace in the eyes of the Lord. This grace produced the physical salvation of the human race through the obedience of one man. In the midst of judgment, the rain that was necessary for trees to spring up was released from heaven, and God showed the human race mercy and grace. Remember Genesis 2:5 says, "for the Lord God had not sent rain on the earth and there was no one to work the ground." But Noah, who found grace in the eyes of the Lord, was prepared to be a body through which God saved the earth from unfruitfulness.

But what then are the trees that God spoke of in Genesis 2:5? God was not concerned with literal trees. Isaiah spoke of trees in this way:

> The Spirit of the Sovereign Lord is on me, because the Lord has anointed me to proclaim good news to the poor. He has sent me to bind up the brokenhearted, to proclaim freedom for the captives and release from darkness for the prisoners, to proclaim the year of the Lord's favor and the day of vengeance of our God, to comfort all who mourn, and provide for those who grieve in Zion—to bestow on them a crown of beauty instead of ashes, the oil of joy instead of mourning, and a garment of praise instead of a spirit of despair. They will be called oaks of righteousness, a planting of the Lord for the display of his splendor. (Isaiah 61:1–3)

The King James Version uses the word *trees* in place of the word *oaks*. These trees of righteousness are people who encounter the saving grace of God through the man who was cultivated for God's use. In other words, God cultivates His people so He can pour out His grace to produce righteousness in other people. God told Solomon, "If my people … will … then I will hear from heaven." This meant that God looks for people who will be cultivated to become His people, and through them He pours out mercy from heaven to earth.

People Who Bear the Name of the Lord

Now that we know what God meant when He spoke of the land, let's move on to the other part of 1 Chronicles 7:14. Though God uses people to restore other people, not anyone will do. God gave Solomon the criteria for the kind of person He seeks to work restoration through. God said, "If My people who are called by My Name." Only God's people who are called by His name qualify to be a vessel of restoration on God's behalf. This leads to the question, "Who are God's people who are called by His name?" Some may say the answer is Christians, or even those who are believers in Jesus. But is it enough to think that as long as people call us Christians or followers of Jesus that we are called by God's name?

Moses wanted to know God more. The scriptures describe his encounter with the Lord in this way: "And the Lord said, "I will cause all my goodness to pass in front of you, and I will proclaim my name, the Lord, in your presence. I will have mercy on whom I will have mercy, and I will have compassion on whom I will have compassion" (Exodus 33:19).

When the Lord passed in front of Moses, the scripture records, "Then the Lord came down in the cloud and stood there with him and proclaimed his name, the Lord. And he passed in front of Moses, proclaiming, "The Lord, the Lord, the compassionate and gracious God, slow to anger, abounding in love and faithfulness, maintaining love to thousands, and forgiving wickedness, rebellion and sin. Yet he does not leave the guilty unpunished; he punishes the children and their children for the sin of the parents to the third and fourth generation" (Exodus 34:5–7). We see, then, that the name of the Lord is associated with His compassion and grace, His patience, kindness, and faithfulness to these ways. The name of the Lord speaks of the mercy of God. So then those who are called by God's name are the people through whom God shows His mercy.

Because God's people are those through whom He shows His mercy to others, what kind of people must God's people be? What kind of character must God's people possess? God explained this to Solomon 2 Chronicles 7:14. They must be humble, prayerful, loyal, and repentant. Such people are cultivated and will be heard by God.

Keys to Access the Healing of Your Land

When the scriptures speak of the healing of our land, it is not simply a quick fix for a problem. The healing of our land comes about by a transformation process that God brings about in His people first and then to others around them. Transformation speaks of a change without intent or desire to change back to the former. This is the healing God spoke of when He said, "I will heal your land." When God heals it is not meant to be momentary but permanent. This is better understood when we see God's healing as a matter of the soul and the healing of the body as a sign of the work within the soul. So the healing of our land is a permanent work God desires to do in us.

God gave us the keys to access the healing of our land and the restoring of a plagued life, even a plagued nation. These keys are:
1. humility (fasting)
2. prayer (communion)
3. seeking God's face (knowing God)
4. turning from wicked ways (repentance, which is changing)

These are given as responsibilities to the people who are called by God's name. All four keys are required for God to hear from heaven and heal our land. I believe that in times past, many have thought that fasting alone would bring healing to the land, but that is not consistent with what the Bible expresses. God set four requirements for us to meet before we can have access to the healing.

Key 1—Humble Yourself with Fasting

Fasting is the ultimate expression of humbling ourselves. To humble yourself is to become submissive to another, just as a lamb submits to be slaughtered. Submission in fasting causes us to have God's attentive ears. But if we fast alone, we will only see the results of submission. Fasting God's way makes us eligible to be heard on high, but this alone will not bring healing from God to a broken land. For land to be cultivated, submission is only the first step.

The book of the Kings gives us an example of one who fasted but did not do the other requirements, and it prevented the healing of his life and nation. King Ahab sinned against the Lord in a greater measure than those before him. He influence Israel into serving a counterfeit master, and so they lived by dead commands. This caused the nation to move itself from being under God's blessing into a curse. Ahab broke God's first two commandments, which are (1) "You shall have no other gods except me," and (2) "You shall not make any graven image of God using something inferior to God."

Ahab's sin in worshiping Baal was quite interesting and unique. The word *Baal* means owner and master, just as Jehovah means Lord and Master. This helped to confuse the people, so they did not know the difference between God and Baal. Because of Ahab, the people served Baal as God. Because the people had a diluted, lifeless view of God, they actually thought that Baal was God. Because Ahab sinned against God in this way, God pronounced judgment upon him. God told him, "I am going to bring disaster on you. I will wipe out your descendants and cut off from Ahab every last male in Israel—slave or free. I will make your house like that of Jeroboam son of Nebat and that of Baasha son of Ahijah, because you have aroused my anger and have caused Israel to sin" (1 Kings 22:21–22). When the prophet Elijah told King Ahab what the Lord's judgment was concerning his sins, the scripture says that Ahab responded with humility and meekness. "When Ahab heard these words, he tore his clothes, put on sackcloth and fasted. He lay in sackcloth and went around meekly" (1 Kings 21:27).

When the Lord saw Ahab's meekness, He showed mercy to Ahab. He turned from a fierce judgment and prolonged Ahab's life. The scripture records God's response to Ahab's humility in this way: "Then the word of the Lord came to Elijah the Tishbite: 'Have you noticed how Ahab has humbled himself before Me? Because he has humbled himself, I will not bring this disaster in his day, but I will bring it on his house in the days of his son'" (1 Kings 21:28–29). It was Ahab's fasting that caused God to repent, just when He was going to bring judgment. Yet is it enough to delay judgment? Was Ahab's land healed? Wouldn't it be better if there had been complete restoration in Ahab's life? Ahab humbled himself, but he did not commune or seek to know the one true God. Ahab held on to his dead perception of who God is, and he remained unhealed.

First Kings 22 speaks of an event when God decided how Ahab should die. God sent Ahab to a place that was once a place of refuge for those who accidentally killed someone. The one who accidentally killed would go there to be protected from the avenger of the dead. But if someone was guilty of murder and fled to such a city, the murderer would be killed by the people in that city. God arranged that Ahab should die in a city of refuge because he did not repent of his wicked ways by seeking to know the true God. He caused so many Israelites to move away from God, who is the source of life, to enter into death and dead works. So when Ahab went to the place of refuge, he died. Though Ahab submitted to God in humility, he clung to Baal, who was the counterfeit god and did not truly turn to know God. He was not restored, and Israel was left scattered.

My friend, be careful that you do not have the same heart as Ahab. Be sure that you do not see God as what you think a master and lord should be like. God is greater than our dead perceptions of Him. Having a dead perception of God and influencing others to have such a view can bring the judgment of God upon your life. Also, do not think that submission through fasting is enough to bring God's healing and fruitfulness to your life. Submission only delays God's judgment long enough for you to get to know God. If you do not take time to know God in prayer, then you will hold on to your dead views. This would only result in your own death from reigning in this life.

Let's see why it's important to pray, which is getting to know God.

Key Number 2—Prayer (Communion with God)

Prayer is our response to a conversation that God initiates by His Spirit. Without God's initiation to commune with Him, we would not seek His will to be done. Instead, we would seek our own interests and, in turn, not pray as we ought. Any prayer that is not in response to God's initial communication to us originates from self, and it is either self-centered or self-righteous at heart. These kinds of prayers often involve a fake display of communion, without any real attempt to engage God. Any who pray in this way never come to know the God to whom they claim to pray. But God, whose name is Merciful, searches for us to influence us into truly seeking Him. God knows our inabilities and sends the Holy Spirit to help us pray as we should.

The apostle Paul lets us know, "In the same way, the Spirit helps us in our weakness. We do not know what we ought to pray for, but the Spirit himself intercedes for us through wordless groans" (Romans 8:26). It is God who helps us have a meaningful and genuine conversation with Him in prayer.

Prayer is reflecting the word of light that the God of heaven sent to earth—that is, prayer is communicating with God about what He has to say concerning the earth. God expects the earth to reflect heaven, but until the light of heaven invades earth, the earth cannot respond to heaven. The prophet Isaiah declared the relationship between heaven and earth: "This is what the Lord says: 'Heaven is my throne, and the earth is my footstool. Where is the house you will build for me? Where will my resting place be?'" (Isaiah 66:1). As the footstool is made to reflect the glory of the throne, so too must the earth reflect the glory of heaven. Since humankind was given dominion over matters of the earth, God expects us to speak on its behalf. To speak concerning the will of God for the earth, on behalf of the earth, is called prayer. Jesus taught us to pray in a way that causes the earth to reflect heaven. He said, "Our Father in heaven, hallowed be your name, your kingdom come, your will be done, on earth as it is in heaven... And lead us not into temptation, but deliver us from the evil one" (Matthew 6:9–10).

When we, to whom God gave dominion over the earth, pray to the God of heaven, we must seek that God will make everything on earth as it is in heaven. To desire any other vision for the things on earth is to oppose God's purpose for the earth He created. This is why we must know God's will and then apply our God-given dominion to request that it be as it is willed in heaven. To do this is to pray.

Prayer, then, is admitting that we desire to see God's will done in our lives. Prayer is the means through which God attains the permission of submissive vessels to bring the kingdom of heaven to earth. If fasting is submission to God, then prayer is the permission given to God to heal our land. When we pray, we give God permission to depose the corrupt character within us. Jesus also taught His disciples to pray this way: "Your kingdom come, your will be done, on earth as it is in heaven... And lead us not into temptation, but deliver us from the evil one" (Matthew 6:10, 13). The evil one does not refer to the devil but to the fleshly nature that accompanies us in the wilderness of sanctification. This evil one is carnal and seeks to please self. It prohibits the blessings of God and the manifestation of the kingdom of heaven on earth. This is why we must pray that we be delivered from the fleshly nature. Also, the word *earth* in this passage does not simply refer to the planet; it mainly refers to God's people. It is from God's people that the impact of the kingdom of heaven will flow to others. Other versions of this verse use the words "in earth," instead of "on earth." *In earth* speaks to the kingdom of heaven being in us. *On earth* refers to the impact the kingdom of heaven makes in this world through those to whom the Kingdom has come. So when we pray the Lord's Prayer, we are asking that God will dispossess the carnality in us and place the heavenly in us, so that we manifest His will and please Him.

If we fast for the healing of our land but do not pray to God, then we are attempting to submit while refusing to admit. We must understand that submitting is validated by admitting. Though King Ahab humbled himself in fasting, he did not validate God's will to show him mercy, so he was not restored. On the other hand, King Manasseh's story gives us an example of one who submitted and admitted, and he saw God's restorative power in his life. The scriptures described his situation this way:

> The Lord spoke to Manasseh and his people, but they paid no attention. So the Lord brought against them the army commanders of the king of Assyria, who took Manasseh prisoner, put a hook in his nose, bound him with bronze shackles and took him to Babylon. In his distress he sought the favor of the Lord his God and humbled himself greatly before the God of his ancestors. And when he prayed to him, the Lord was moved by his entreaty and listened to his plea; so he brought him back to Jerusalem and to his kingdom. Then Manasseh knew that the Lord is God. (2 Chronicles 33:11–13)

This is so much better than what Ahab did, who, when he sinned and God proclaimed a judgment, humbled himself, and God only delayed the judgment. But because Manasseh fasted and sought the Lord in prayer, he was not merely spared of judgment but was restored to his kingdom. His corrupted character changed from one who did not acknowledge the Lord to one who realized the Lord alone is God. The wonderful thing about a healed character is that it brings healing to others who have sick character. Manasseh's healing resulted in the reformation of Israel. The people were taught to serve the Lord and not to serve other gods. This means that when we humble ourselves and pray, seek the Lord, and turn from wicked ways, we can experience a change within us that God uses to influence others to come to Him. God heals us first so that we can be used to heal others.

Key3—Seeking God's Face (Knowing God)

"The eyes of the Lord are on the righteous, and his ears are attentive to their cry; but the face of the Lord is against those who do evil, to blot out their name from the earth" (Psalm 34:15–16).

The face plays a very important role during communication with another person; it is used to express our thoughts or feelings to another. We use our faces to display expressions of internal opinions. In the scriptures we find written expressions relating to God's face, which help us understand His mind and heart. When the scriptures say that God's eyes are on someone, or His ear is attentive to someone, it is usually a good thing. This is similar to saying that God's face is toward someone in approval. But when God turns a blind eye or a deaf ear to someone, it is like turning His face away from that person in disapproval. To have God's face turned toward us speaks of having His favor and grace. This is why we must strive to know of what God approves and disapproves and do what pleases Him.

The expressions of God's face tell us more than that which he approves and disapproves; they also tell us who He is. God's face can only express what is inside Him, and God is righteous at heart. The scripture above states, "The eyes of the Lord are on the righteous." The Lord expresses approval of righteousness because He is righteous. This is why those who live righteous before Him receive His favor. But because no one can be righteous in his or her own strength, no one can receive God's approval on his or her own. This is why those who desire that God make them righteous receive God's approval. This is the same as saying God approves of those who seek His righteousness. When God told Solomon, "If My people would … seek My face," it's like saying, "If My people would seek My righteousness."

The only way we can see and know God's righteousness is for God to show and tell us. This is why the Word of God was manifested as Jesus to make us righteous. The apostle Paul stated, "God made him who had no sin to be sin for us, so that in him we might become the righteousness of God" (2 Corinthians 5:21). Though the Son of God was not made because He was in the beginning with God, He was made flesh to reveal who God is to humankind. Through Him, it was made possible for people to see the Father's heart and become righteous. Through Jesus Christ, we all can experience His face of approval.

Ignoring God due to ignorance of God led to a cursed life, so the healing of cursed lives will come by knowing God. When I was a little boy, I had a T-shirt with the words "To know me is to love me" written on the front. I didn't understand what it meant then, but now I see truth in those words. To get to know someone is to pursue intimacy or closeness with that person. This takes getting to know what is on the inside and not just his or her externals expressions. To get inside someone's heart requires love for that person. This is true with God—to experience God's heart requires that we love God with everything we have. This is what it means to seek God's face. This is what it means to want to know Him. So the words God spoke to Solomon can be interpreted this way: "If My people who are called by My name would get to know Me, they would love Me."

Key 4—Turn from Your Wicked Ways (Repentance)

Notice that God gave four keys that lead to three responses. The four keys are (1) humbling yourself, (2) praying, (3) seeking God's face, and (4) turning from wicked ways—these are our responsibilities. The three responses God gives us when we do the four keys are (1) hear from heaven, (2) forgive our sins, and (3) heal our land. There is a correlation between God's three responses to our four responsibilities, but the correlation is not written respectively. For God to hear us, we must humble ourselves; for God to forgive us, we must turn from our wicked ways; and for God to heal our land, we must pray and seek His face.

I bring this up so that we will notice that God's actions to our obedience is not sequential, but it is best seen as a package deal. If we provide all four keys in obedience to God, He will respond with all three. The reason is very simple: God is saying that we must humble ourselves in submission to Him, so He can engage us in a conversation with Him in prayer. As we commune with Him in prayer, God reveals Himself to us. God knows that at the sight of Him, we will change from who we used to be to who we were created to be; that is a fruitful land.

As we engage God in submission, He hears us, forgives us, and restores us. God's forgiveness is expressed in an earlier order than our repentance. In the four responsibilities given to us, repentance is last on the list. By looking at the order of things, it would appear as if God forgives us before we repent. The truth is God *does* forgive us before we repent, but if we do not repent before it is too late, we will continue on the path of destruction and will perish.

Oh, how wonderful our God is that He forgives us before we even repent. This is so much like God, just as He expressed through Jesus on the cross, when He said, "'Father, forgive them, for they do not know what they are doing.' And they divided up his clothes by casting lots" (Luke 23:34). Jesus was asking God to forgive the people while they were killing Him, not when they were repenting. God has no trouble forgiving our sins in advance of our repentance, but we have trouble receiving forgiveness.

In order to receive the blessings that God, in His mercy, has already prepared for us, we must be transformed at the sight of Him. We must encounter God before we can turn from our wicked ways. Sir Isaac Newton, an English physicist, worded a mathematical law of motion. He said, "An object at rest stays at rest and an object in motion stays in motion with the same speed and in the same direction unless acted upon by an Unbalanced Force." This law means that if something is stagnant or is moving in a certain direction, it will remain stagnant or continue to go in the direction it is going, unless it encounters a force that is different than the force it is experiencing. This is what is meant by an unbalanced force—a force that brings an unbalance to the state of the object. This force is similar to God's work to get us from being stagnant or to change the direction we are going so we go in another direction. It is only by God's force that we can change the direction we are going and move in the right direction. We must encounter God's force so that we can repent. Yet God must forgive us before He heals our land.

The word *repent* is formed from two words. One word is the prefix *re*, and the other word is *penitent*. Penitent means "feeling or showing sorrow and regret for having done wrong" (merriam-webster.com). *Re* means "back to the original place, also with the sense of undoing" (etymology.com). The two parts together give us *re-penitent*, or *repent*, which is the feeling and showing of sorrow and regret for sin and pursuing possible means undo and go back to the original state. This is why every true message you hear about repentance always speaks of turning from the direction in which you were going to go in another. Turning is crucial in repentance; it is the only way you can change the direction you were going.

Let's submit ourselves to God, so that as we encounter Him in prayer, He will cause us to turn from wicked, rebellious way. When we encounter God, we will be transformed from vessels of unrighteousness to vessels of righteousness. This is the change that we need that will please God. As God said, "If My people will ... Turn from their wicked ways, then will I ... forgive their sins and heal their land."

CHAPTER 6

Fasting for Restoration

Now that we have a better understanding of the true purpose of fasting and how it works, let's look at its application in ministry. Every ministry that is given to us by God involves restoration of some sort. God uses people and gives them ministries to pour out His grace in our lives and to deliver to us what we need. There is a propaganda of the devil that only titled ministers had ministries. This lie infiltrated the church and debilitated many, but this is so far from the truth. For we know that anyone who obeys God to do anything good for another or to help others in any way has ministered in some way. It does not matter how small or insignificant it may seem; it is doing God's will that makes us His ministers.

With regard to fasting, in scripture there is a direct connection to fasting and God's restorative work. All who minister must see that connection and incorporate it in their ministries. True ministry that is from God carries the love of God, for God is love. Since fasting expresses the greatest love someone can show for another, then anyone who ministers should include fasting at times. If we all would willingly offer up the sacrifice of fasting with our ministering, no matter how insignificant it may seem, our ministering would have much greater effectiveness.

Fasting Identifies Your Allegiance in Ministry

Do you not know, brothers and sisters—for I am speaking
to those who know the law—that the law has authority

over someone only as long as that person lives? For example, by law a married woman is bound to her husband as long as he is alive, but if her husband dies, she is released from the law that binds her to him. So then, if she has sexual relations with another man while her husband is still alive, she is called an adulteress. But if her husband dies, she is released from that law and is not an adulteress if she marries another man. (Romans 7:1–3 NIV)

The death that the apostle Paul spoke of in the passage above was used as an analogy of the disconnection between a believer in Jesus Christ and his or her selfish will. Fasting is one of the acts that expresses this death and disconnection. A woman whose husband is still alive is not free to become one with another man. But if the husband dies, then that woman is free to be in union with another man. In the same way, fasting expresses the death of our own works and the union we once had with the will of the flesh. This expression of death to the flesh also signifies that a legal union now exists between us and the Lord. Through fasting, God can legally bind His will to ours.

Fasting is also a sign of death to the old ministry while aligning ourselves with God's ministry. Fasting expresses dying to the old cravings to please the flesh, while taking up a new desire to please God. It is the death we go through in fasting that makes us ready for ministry. Jesus taught, "None is able to serve two lords, for either he will hate the one and love the other, or he will hold to the one, and despise the other; ye are not able to serve God and Mammon" (Matthew 6:24 Young's Literal Translation). In the same way, we cannot be ministers of God and ministers of selfish desires. We either will do what God wants us to do or what we want to do. This is why it's necessary that the will of the flesh die so that we might be freed from its grasp to do the will of God.

Ministry Begins with Fasting

Since all ministries increases their effectiveness by the death that comes from fasting, how much more should those who are called to public ministry begin their ministry with fasting. Fasting at the beginning of your ministry would be like ensuring that you start the race on the right foot. The Old Testament gave us a great description of the start of Israel's ministry as a nation. Israel's ministry was the most public ministry mentioned in Scripture because they were to be ministers to all the nations of the world. After they crossed the Red Sea, God told them, "You will be for me a kingdom of priests and a holy nation" (Exodus 19:6 NIV). This was Israel's call to public ministry. God used Israel to minister to the world by making them a conduit through which the Savior of the world would come. Because of Israel's ministry, today all the nations of the earth has heard or will hear about God's mighty power to deliver those who trust Him.

As a nation, Israel began it's ministry with a sacrificial death—the death of the lamb broke the chains of Pharaoh, and Israel was free to serve God, just as He commanded. This death represents the death of our Lord Jesus Christ, who died on the cross for our sins. But before Israel could become the ministers they were called to be, they had to undergo another death. God needed the people to die to their own will so that they might receive His. This death was carried out when they fasted in the wilderness. It was only after they fasted in the wilderness that they were ready to enter the Promised land and engage effective ministry.

Moses described a fast that Israel experienced in the wilderness when he told them, "Remember how the LORD your God led you through the wilderness for these forty years, humbling you and testing you to prove your character, and to find out whether or not you would obey his commands. Yes, he humbled you by letting you go hungry and then feeding you with manna, a food previously unknown to you and your ancestors. He did it to teach you that people do not live by bread alone; rather, we live by every word that comes from the mouth of the LORD" (Deuteronomy 8:2–3 NLT). God led Israel into a forty-day fast, which, because of stubbornness, became a forty-year fast. The purpose of the fast was so that God would realign Israel's heart to His will. When they were in Egypt, their ministry was one of self-preservation, but that ministry led them to futility. Now that they were freed to serve the Lord by the death of the lamb, God led them to fast so that they might die to that old way of thinking and ministering. He did this so that the nation of Israel might be equip for the ministry ahead of them. Israel did not know how to be effective ministers in the world so God had to reveal how. This was represented by the manna He gave them in the wilderness. Manna, which means "what is it", symbolized what is unknown, or the revelation of God. No minister of God could effectively carry out the will of God without having the revelation of God.

Some believe that fasting is not necessary to live pleasing to God, and they treat fasting as merely a physical work of restraint. Such people have missed the purpose God has set for fasting with regard to their own will, refusing to express the sacrifice that He requires. But consider this: when the nation of Israel refused to fast in the wilderness, this expressed the stubbornness of their hearts. In refusing to fast, they tested the Lord and were not allowed to enter the land of promise until their stubbornness was broken. This can be us if we refuse to fast when the Lord is leading us into it. Stubbornness, by refusing to fast, will only delay us from truly entering into our calling and inheritance. This hinders our ministry by weakening the impact we were meant to make in the world.

Restoration Starts with Separation

Separation from God brought the beautiful world into darkness, and separation from this world will restore it to its created beauty. When I say "this world," I do not mean the trees, grass, rivers, sea, mountains. and so on, that would be only a part of the world. The world is not just the earth, but it is a system. The world system that God created and made was made up of His Word, His Spirit, the man He created and made, and the earth that the man was placed in to dominate it like God would. When God was at the head of this system, the system was full of potential and was heading to great success. But when the man sided with Satan, the world system changed philosophies and direction. The system was disconnected from its true life source, lost its true potential, and went off course from its true destiny.

Sin separated the world from God and cast a shadow on it, preventing it from reflecting heaven's system. This was the created purpose for the world, to reflect the system of heaven. But the system that remained after man sinned was separated from God unto itself to self-exist. Sadly, anything that separates itself from its purpose is separated for destruction.

This is like a cell phone that is separated from the service provider; it eventually will sit on the shelf or in a drawer. Because it is not being used for its intended purpose, it will soon to be discarded. The same can happen to a self-existing worldly system that does not fulfill its created purpose. But "God so loved the world, that he gave his only begotten Son, that whosoever believeth in him should not perish, but have everlasting life" (John 3:16 KJV).

I must clarify that God does not love this self-existing system that the god of this world dominates and promulgates. This system finds its philosophies from and is governed by the devil. The devil, who is Satan, was the first to separate himself in order to self-exist for selfish reasons. Isaiah wrote about Satan, saying, "How you are fallen from heaven, O shining star, son of the morning! You have been thrown down to the earth, you who destroyed the nations of the world. For you said to yourself, 'I will ascend to heaven and set my throne above God's stars. I will preside on the mountain of the gods far away in the north. I will climb to the highest heavens and be like the Most High.' Instead, you will be brought down to the place of the dead, down to its lowest depths" (Isaiah 14:12–15 NLT).

Satan (which means adversary) separated himself from God's created purpose for his life; he did this for selfish reasons. This caused him to embrace a destiny that would lead him straight for destruction. Justly, all the other angels who followed Satan were also set on this path. In time, Satan became the god of this world through trickery. The current world system finds its beginnings in Satan and his deceptive lie through the serpent in the garden of Eden. Rightfully, he is called the devil, which means deceiver. When Adam submitted to his temptations and lies, he handed over dominion of the heavenly mandate to the adversary. Under his leadership the world would only be plunged into destruction. Through Adam's submission, the devil began to dominate the system of the world to promote his agenda. The devil's worldly system allows anyone to do what he or she wants to do, as long as it pleases himself or herself. Just as Satan is about his own will and selfish desires, the sinful world system is all about self. Unfortunately, just as Satan and his demonic hoards are set for destruction, any person who follows them and refuses to repent will also be destroyed. This is why those who want to be a part of what God is doing in the earth must separate himself or herself from this current worldly system. Anyone who does not separate himself or herself from this sinful worldly system cannot carry out the will of God.

The world that God "so loved" refers to the system I mentioned earlier, where He partners with mankind to dominate the earth with fruitful blessings. This world system that God loves is made up of people who are made in His image and likeness by the Spirit of God and the Word of God. Those who are filled with God's Spirit and Word are suitable to carry out God's will in the earth. Such people are used by God so that He can make the world system just like the system of heaven. God ought to preside on the earth in the same way He in presides in heaven. But God chose to preside on the earth through people, and in doing so, God can use the system of the world to make the earth like heaven. So He declared through the prophet Isaiah, "This is what the Lord says: Heaven is my throne, and the earth is my footstool. Where is the house you will build for me? Where will my resting place be?" (Isaiah 66:1 NIV). Unfortunately, since the world was corrupted by the devil, God could not use the system of the world in the state it was in. For this reason, because God so loved the world, He is restoring it.

The presence of the Holy Spirit is crucial in the ministry of restoration, for it is through His presence that the world can become the system that God intended in creation. God saw the great blessing humankind could be if they would have the indwelling presence of the Holy Spirit. He was so convinced of this that He sent His only begotten Son, the Word of God, to die in order to prepare the means through which the Holy Spirit could come to mankind. The presence of the Holy Spirit makes humans like God—it is His Spirit in us that allows God to rule on the earth, thus making the earth His footstool.

The Holy Spirit also transforms people into ministers of God through His presence to guide and power to work. To minister is to serve God and work on His agenda. God's agenda is to restore the hearts of men to their created purpose—to bring the world (system) to the end He desired when He created it. And as His ministers in the world, we are to serve and help restore people to godliness. We do this when we love others through offering up our lives unto God as a living sacrifice, just as Jesus did. Jesus speaks of service in this way: "But whoever would be great among you must be your servant, and whoever would be first among you must be slave of all. For even the Son of Man came not to be served but to serve, and to give his life as a ransom for many" (Mark 10:43–45 ESV).

Seeing that Jesus, who is our Lord and Master, lived a life of serving and blessing others, we who believe in Him must live the same way. Our purpose for living must be like Jesus's purpose, which is to serve all and to give our lives as a ransom for many. Though our ransom is used by God in different ways, through Jesus the result of our ransom brings about salvation in some sort to others. Ransoms are for the purpose of purchasing back someone who was stolen, which results in salvation to the one who was lost. We are now separated so that our lives will be blessed by God to have the value required to ransom those who are lost.

God Commands Us to Be Separated

To be used in the work of the Lord to bring restoration on the earth we must first be separated from our previous father's house and family. Jesus said to those who did not believe Him, "You belong to your father, the devil, and you want to carry out your father's desires. He was a murderer from the beginning, not holding to the truth, for there is no truth in him. When he lies, he speaks his native language, for he is a liar and the father of lies" (John 8:44 NIV). We are to be separated from the devil and his family before we can minister to others. We find this call for separation when God called Abraham. The scripture says, "The Lord had said to Abram, "Go from your country, your people and your father's household to the land I will show you. "I will make you into a great nation, and I will bless you; I will make your name great, and you will be a blessing. I will bless those who bless you, and whoever curses you I will curse; and all peoples on earth will be blessed through you"" (Genesis 12:1–3 NIV).

In Genesis 12, we see where God issued the command for separation to Abraham for the ministry of establishing covenantal blessings. God poured out promises upon Abraham and used him as a medium through which God would pass on those promises, so that anyone who would believe as Abraham did would also receive the blessed promises. God desires to use everyone who will believe Him as Abraham did and obey the command of separating themselves to bring some kind of blessing to the world. Fasting is one of the ways we obey this command of separating ourselves, even from our self-driven desires in this world. Fasting from natural food represents a separation from the things that people crave in the world, and it exchanges those cravings for the will of God. It also represents a separation from what we think we need to live in this world.

Separation from the world has been God's requirement for His chosen people in order to first bless them and then bless others through them. The same thing can be said about fasting, for it is one of God's required means of being blessed to be a blessing. It is not that God wants His people to not live in the world; rather, He wants us to live victoriously in it. This requires being in it but separated from it—in a sense, dead to its influence. Fasting facilitates this requirement.

The apostle Paul expounded on this in a passage from the book of Isaiah: "Therefore, "Come out from them and be separate, says the Lord. Touch no unclean thing, and I will receive you"" (2 Corinthians 6:17 NIV). This separation is a separation from the systemic philosophies of this world and its pleasures. Those who are separated by God are called to disassociate themselves from the negative influences of the world. Only when we live victoriously over these debilitating influences can we be blessings to those around us.

God's command to be separate from this world does not conclude with the physical departure from this world, but there are some cases when we must physically remove ourselves from the situation. It was the same apostle Paul who told the Corinthian church how we are to carry out this separation. He said, "I wrote to you in my letter not to associate with sexually immoral people—not at all meaning the people of this world who are immoral, or the greedy and swindlers, or idolaters. In that case you would have to leave this world. But now I am writing to you that you must not associate with anyone who claims to be a brother or sister but is sexually immoral or greedy, an idolater or slanderer, a drunkard or swindler. Do not even eat with such people" (1 Corinthians 5:9–11 NIV). This commandment from the Lord through the apostle is a hard pill to swallow, and many have frankly refused to live by it. But God commands this for our own good. When the apostle stated, "In that case you would have to leave this world," he was letting us know that separation was not a command to physically leave this world. But when he said, "You must not associate with anyone who claims to be a brother or sister but is sexually immoral or greedy, an idolater or slanderer, a drunkard or swindler," he was telling us to not be associated with those who claim to be separate but are not. We are told to physically remove ourselves from such control of sin. No one who is under the control of sin will ever bring restoration to people who are bound to sin. For this reason we must be physically active in separating ourselves from sin's control. Fasting is also physical action that show our physical removal from the cravings of the sinful worldly system in order to be used by God. This physical act actually frees us from being under the control of worldly system to please ourselves.

Fasting Reveals God's Strategies for Restoration

Restoration is needed only when things are broken or ruined. When humankind sinned against God, the world was ruined and in need of restoration. God called His servants to be conduits through whom He brought the grace for restoration upon the earth. Every servant He chose was called to be separated from the ways of the world—they even had to die to their own desires to fulfill their calling. Through them, God gave His Word that brings healing. Today we benefit from the death that many before us have endured. When we were still in sin, Jesus died for us. Not only did Jesus die, but all those who died to themselves also died for our sake. Through their deaths, we received God's grace that restores.

Fasting is also a death that we endure, so that those who are a part of this world's system can come to know God or at least to know of Him. Therefore, those He chooses to be agents of His grace must be willing to lay down their lives not for the righteous, but for sinners in this world. Remember, it is not the righteous that needs restoration, but the ones who fall short of God's glory. There is a parable about the kingdom of heaven that describes it as a man who bought a whole field so that he could have the pearl in it. We must be willing to pay the price for the whole field at times, just so we can see a precious soul come to repentance.

The prophet Elijah was one of God's servants who God used to pour out the grace of restoration from a false view of God. In his time, the nation of Israel was divided into two kingdoms—the kingdom of Judah and the kingdom of Israel. Elijah was sent to be a minister in the kingdom of Israel because they had the wrong view of who God is. The kingdom of

Israel turned from worshiping YHWH (YaHWeH or JeHoWaH known as Jehovah) to worshiping Baal. Interestingly, the word *Jehovah* which was derived from a combination of the word *YHWH* and the word *Adonai* which means Lord, Master, and Owner. Whereas the Hebrew word *Baal* means lord, master, and husband. Though the meanings of these two names appear to be the same, they were far from it. Jehovah was Owner, by right, of being their Creator, the I AM, whereas Baal was Israel's husband by their choice. By making Baal their husband, the kingdom of Israel made Baal their lord and master. We see, then, that it was a false view of who God is that led them to think that Baal was God. But we must learn from their lives that God is not who we choose Him to be, for He is who He is.

God chose the prophet Elijah to represent God's zeal to make His people know who He really is. This made Elijah's ministry a representation of the spirit of restoration. This is why the prophet Malachi referred to him and said, "See, I will send the prophet Elijah to you before that great and dreadful day of the LORD comes. He will turn the hearts of the parents to their children, and the hearts of the children to their parents; or else I will come and strike the land with total destruction" (Malachi 4:5–6 NIV). Because Malachi said this after Elijah was taken to heaven, he was speaking of the spirit of Elijah. I believe that God's zeal for restoration is not complete, and that is why Elijah did not die but was taken into heaven. This means that God can send the spirit of Elijah to the earth over and over, for this zeal of the Lord did not die with him. The scriptures tell us about Elijah's fast.

> Elijah was afraid and ran for his life. When he came to Beersheba in Judah, he left his servant there, while he himself went a day's journey into the wilderness. He came to a broom bush, sat down under it and prayed that he might die. "I have had enough, LORD," he said. "Take my life; I am no better than my ancestors." Then he lay down under the bush and fell asleep. All at once an angel touched him and said, "Get up and eat." He looked around, and there by his head was some bread baked over hot coals, and a jar of water. He ate and drank and then lay down again. The angel of the LORD came back a second

time and touched him and said, "Get up and eat, for the journey is too much for you." So he got up and ate and drank. Strengthened by that food, he traveled forty days and forty nights until he reached Horeb, the mountain of God. There he went into a cave and spent the night." (1 King 19:3–8 NIV)

Let me set the stage that led up to Elijah's fast. The Lord instructed Elijah to confront the work of Baal in Israel by putting the power of Baal to the test in front of the people. Elijah anticipated that this would be the final blow that God would use to destroy Baal's work in the land. He must have thought that as soon as the people saw that Baal was false and powerless, everything would be restored to the way it should be. It was Elijah and his God against 450 priests of Baal and their god. Elijah and his God won a great victory over the prophets of Baal, and the people acknowledged that the Lord is God. But when Jezebel, the queen, heard about this, she swore that she would kill Elijah.

Before we bash Elijah in our minds over his reaction to Jezebel's threat, just remember that Elijah spent three years avoiding Ahab and Jezebel because they were killing prophets of God. The only reason Elijah survived was because the Lord told him where to hide. To hide for another unknown amount of time would have been a hardship repeated, and then the Lord didn't tell Elijah to hide this time, so it might have seemed he was about to face an even greater trial. I can only image how Elijah felt when he asked the Lord to take his life. Elijah made an interesting statement when he said, "I am no better than my ancestors who have already died." This reminds me of Moses with the people in the wilderness. They demonstrated great stubbornness of heart by refusing to believe God's mighty deeds. It may have seemed the same to Elijah when Jezebel threatened his life, insinuating that she would reestablish what was just destroyed and render his efforts as useless. Just as Moses died without being able to bring the people to the place of promise, Elijah may have thought he had failed and asked to die. But God wanted to show Elijah that this was the opportune time to fast for strategies for restoration.

At a glance, it may seem like the forty-day fast Elijah went on was not productive, but I beg to differ. God was showing mercy to Israel through

Elijah's ministry, but since Elijah was discouraged, God set Elijah on a fast that resulted in the selection of successors to complete the task. This is how it happened: Elijah received food from God that gave him the strength to go on a fast for forty days and nights. Elijah took it upon himself to go to Mount Sinai in a cave, but God asked him what he was doing there! Elijah complained before the Lord about the work of the ministry, so the Lord attempted to teach him by telling him to meet Him at the mouth of the cave. The Lord caused a wind, fire, and a shaking to pass at the front of the mountain, but He did not allow His presence to be in those things. Elijah discerned that the Lord's presence was not in those things, and he did not move. Then the Lord whispered, and Elijah recognized the presence of God in the whisper, so he went to the mouth of the cave. The Lord asked him the same question as before, but Elijah complained again, and the Lord respected his complaint. Elijah thought he was the only one left with zeal for God, but he did not see that the Lord was moving in Israel. It was through His whispers, however, and not though the mighty wind, fire, and shaking. So the Lord reminded Elijah that there were other prophets in Israel who had not submitted or loved Baal. And at the end of the encounter, God gave Elijah a strategy to remove Baal from the land.

The scriptures about Elijah's ministry stands as a template for how we can see the name of God restored by our ministries. One thing we must learn from Elijah is that after God has prepared us to be His representative, fasting can release the strategies He has for restoration through our ministries. Remember that in the season of preparation and fasting, the restoration process may seem nonexistent. But don't lose heart, for God will eventually raise up the Hazaels, Jehus, and Elishas to carry out the works that result in restoration. Remember that restoration starts with separation, and fasting is the death to self that comes after separation. Only when self is dead could the manifested work of restoration really begin.

As I've studied the Bible and listened to the revelations that the Holy Spirit gives me, I have found a common truth in scripture. God consistently shows us the appropriate journey on which we must embark and complete to experience the necessary restoration in our lives. Regarding false belief, God used Elijah to show us the journey to restoration. From his life we learn that in order to be empowered to reveal God in the midst of falsehood, preparation for the baptism of the Holy Spirit and fire is crucial—for the

God who answers by fire, He is God. After we see the baptism of fire, then we experience the rain of God's Word that blesses and makes our lives fruitful. We will have the privilege to ask for the rain in prayer and receive it. But after we have been baptized by His Spirit and have received the showers of His promises to bless, the next thing we need is strategy for manifestation of the blessing. This is where fasting comes in.

Unfortunately, like those who go on trips without maps or assemble furniture without following the instructions, many skip this step and get lost along the way. When we refuse to live a life of fasting, we attempt to skip the part where we seek God for strategy for the work to which He calls us. In the word Elijah received from the Lord after he fasted, God referred to three people He planned to use to remove Baal from Israel. The first mentioned was Hazael as king of Syria, second was Jehu as king of Israel, and third was Elisha as His prophet. The thing I found strange in the word the Lord gave Elijah was that He intended to use the king of Syria to help remove Baal from the land. What made it more interesting was that the person God intended to use was Hazael, the servant of Ben-Hadad, the king of Syria. But when Ben-Hadad was ill, he sent Hazael to Elisha to ask God if he would recover from the sickness. In that conversation with Elisha and Hazael, Elisha told Hazael that he would become king of Syria. Elisha then revealed to Hazael the manner in which he would treat the people of Israel. The scripture describes it this way:

> So Hazael went to meet him, and took a present with him, all kinds of goods of Damascus, forty camels' loads. When he came and stood before him, he said, "Your son Ben-hadad king of Syria has sent me to you, saying, 'Shall I recover from this sickness?'" And Elisha said to him, "Go, say to him, 'You shall certainly recover,' but the LORD has shown me that he shall certainly die." And he fixed his gaze and stared at him, until he was embarrassed. And the man of God wept. And Hazael said, "Why does my lord weep?" He answered, "Because I know the evil that you will do to the people of Israel. You will set on fire their fortresses, and you will kill their young men with the sword and dash in pieces their little ones and rip open

their pregnant women." And Hazael said, "What is your servant, who is but a dog, that he should do this great thing?" Elisha answered, "The LORD has shown me that you are to be king over Syria." (2 Kings 8:9–13 ESV)

This was the same Hazael that the Lord told Elijah He would use to remove Baal from the land. It may seem strange that God would include such an evil person like Hazael in His strategy to remove the false view of God from the hearts of His people. But God used Hazael to demonstrate how the kings of this world are used to remove the seed and the system of false belief. Through the hardship Hazael brought to Israel, God allowed him to participate in rebuilding the trust Israel should have in God. We must not forget that God revealed this ruler through fasting. One of the mistakes that we make as Christians is to think that God is the Christian God, as if He is not almighty God over all people. But God Himself declared, "Although the whole earth is mine, you will be for me a kingdom of priests and a holy nation" (Exodus 19:5–6 NIV). It is not that we belong to God, and the rest of the people on earth belong to Satan. God is Jehovah, the Owner of all humankind—He can use unbelievers to assist His purposes. Though many have pledge allegiance to Satan to follow him, he does not own them. They are only married to him by choice. But thanks be to our God who gives us strategies when we fast. For when we fast, God reveals how He will dissolve the false unions between people and Satan.

As ministers who seek the restoration of the hearts of God's children back to their Father, we must be willing to accept that God uses people in authority in this world to push that agenda. When God chooses a ruler, he or she is not always as we would like the person to be, but the person is always what God needs him or her to be. This speaks specifically to people who rule in government, especially as prime ministers or presidents. Many believers have the idea that they must simply seek the best person, whose morals appear to match their own. But that is not the way God told us to participate in the selection of a ruler. We must keep in mind that no person can be a ruler of another person unless submission is involved. In the same way, anyone who forms an allegiance with a ruler, either by selecting or voting for the person or desiring to have the person rule, will share in the ruler's decisions. For this reason, we should seek God first in fasting to know His strategy and to see whom He desires to work through to bring glory to His name. In doing this, we first make God our King and ruler, becoming participants in the restoration of His glory in the hearts of others through the acts of the ruler He chooses. When we understand this, it is not difficult to fast with a purpose, that God will reveal the ruler through whom He is going to bring glory to His name.

Let's be willing to get involved in fasting, not only for the issues we see in our congregations but in the world around us. Let's adopt the habit of fasting before elections so that we can know the person God is choosing. Let's not promote our own ideas and beliefs without first seeking God's Word and revelation to believe in. I'm not trying to disrupt the election process of any form of government, nor am I trying to promote rebellion against any governmental system. I am attempting to reveal God's power to do good in the world, using the system that is in the world.

The apostle Peter said, "Submit yourselves for the Lord's sake to every human authority: whether to the emperor, as the supreme authority, or to governors, who are sent by him to punish those who do wrong and to commend those who do right. For it is God's will that by doing good you should silence the ignorant talk of foolish people. Live as free people, but do not use your freedom as a cover-up for evil; live as God's slaves. Show proper respect to everyone, love the family of believers, fear God, honor the emperor" (1 Peter 2:13–17 NIV).

Notice the apostle said, "Submit yourself for the Lord's sake." Though we should give our allegiance to God for His glory, we submit to the person He places to rule. How much better would it be if we would side with God on the selection of the person He wants to use? This way, we can see all that God is doing through the ruler to cause men to learn to trust God again, despite their errors, mistakes, and, in some cases, wicked intentions.

Public Ministry Began with Fasting

The other people that God chose to use to remove Baal worship from Israel were Jehu, as king of Israel, and Elisha, as prophet in place of Elijah. God said that whoever Jehu did not destroy, Elisha would destroy. As these men were carrying out God's plan to destroy Baal, we see Jehu removing the people who were promoting Baal worship, but Elisha performed miracles that signified the restoration from dead beliefs.

Elisha performed many miracles by the power of God, but in all of them we see the message that God is jealous to restore the relationship He was meant to have with His people. Had Elijah not fasted, he would not have known of Elisha, whom God chose to carry on the work that he started. Many times ministers think only of themselves and not of those whom God is preparing to carry on the work they started. Many times those who are selected are chosen by means other than by consulting God in prayer and fasting. It is my hope that those who read this book and are in such a position will adopt the ways of Elijah. Fasting reveals God's strategy for ministry. This includes what He is doing and through whom He will do it.

Public ministries, as we know them today, are given to those the Lord wants to give as gifts to the church for edification. Today we have an extension of such ministries, expressed in various forms. For instance, the people who lead worship in song are like pastors who encourage the congregation into a time of cooperative declaration and adoration to God. Though they don't function as a pastor—who, like a shepherd, expresses God's nurturing love to the people of God—they do share a part of the pastor's ministry unto God to encourage and lead.

Another ministry that is not mentioned as part of what we call the fivefold ministry but is a sublet of it is the missionary. A missionary goes out with the intent to deliver the Word of God to those who are outside of the congregation. Missionaries share commonality with evangelists. There are many other ministries that we have labeled today that were not mentioned among the five stated in scripture. This is strictly for identification of duties, for the sake of order in the congregation. Every one of these ministries, from the smallest subset to the ones mentioned explicitly in scripture, must begin with fasting.

The first example we have of a ministry beginning with fasting is the ministry of our Savior and Lord Jesus Christ. In the gospels that express the humanity of Jesus, we see the account of Jesus being led into the wilderness to fast, but in the book of John, this is not mentioned. In this book the emphasis was on the divinity of Jesus as the Son of God, but the Gospel of Matthew emphasized His earthly authority as King. The Gospel of Mark emphasized his submissiveness to God as a servant. The Gospel according to Luke emphasized His earthly compassion as a man.

These three gospels refer to Jesus Christ's humanity. And in His humanity, He fasted. In the same way, we, who are humans, must fast as Jesus did when we begin our ministry. The account given to us was that as soon as Jesus was baptized by John in the Jordan River, He went into the wilderness to fast. The scriptures said that after He fasted, angels came and ministered to Him. The attendance of angels speaks of the strategies that Jesus was given after He fasted. The book of Hebrews reveals this about the angels: "For since the message spoken through angels was binding, and every violation and disobedience received its just punishment, how shall we escape if we ignore so great a salvation? This salvation, which was first announced by the Lord, was confirmed to us by those who heard him" (Hebrew 2:2–3 NIV).

Stephen referred to this before he was stoned. "Was there ever a prophet your ancestors did not persecute? They even killed those who predicted the coming of the Righteous One. And now you have betrayed and murdered him—you who have received the law that was given through angels but have not obeyed it" (Acts 7:52–53 NIV). Stephen explicitly stated that the law was given by angels, referring to the message spoken through angels as stated in the book of Hebrews. From this we see that God delivered His commands through angels. If you are about to enter into ministry, fast as Jesus did before He entered into ministry. Now your fast does not have to specifically be a forty-day fast. But you must be sure to fast so that you can receive the commands of God for your commission.

The scriptures also record how the apostle Paul was set forth in ministry. In the book of Acts, it was recorded: "Now there were in the church that was at Antioch certain prophets and teachers; as Barnabas, and Simeon that was called Niger, and Lucius of Cyrene, and Manaen, which had been brought up with Herod the tetrarch, and Saul. As they ministered to the Lord, and fasted, the Holy Ghost said, Separate me Barnabas and Saul for the work whereunto I have called them. And when they had fasted and prayed, and laid their hands on them, they sent them away" (Acts 13:1–3 KJV).

It was during a fast that the Holy Spirit called the apostle Paul and Barnabas, who were already prophets and teachers, to the special ministry.

This is a testimony to us that though we are already in service for the Lord, in times of fasting the Lord will call us to greater effectiveness in ministry. Notice that it was not mentioned that they were on a forty-day fast when they received the call to this special ministry. This tells us that the amount of day in which they fasted was not the issue when it pertains to being called into the ministry. But we must also be careful to notice that the result of this fast was the call and not the commands and strategies, as received by Jesus after His forty-day fast. Their fast was one that resulted in knowing their calling to greater ministry.

If you have been struggling with knowing what special call God has on your life, then fast and pray and seek God to know, and as surely as He revealed it to the apostles Paul and Barnabas, He will reveal it to you. We all are called to some special ministry, just as we all are special.

Even elders in the church were chosen through times of fasting. The book of Acts recorded, "And when they had ordained them elders in every church, and had prayed with fasting, they commended them to the Lord, on whom they believed" (Acts 14:23 KJV). Fasting was included in the commendations of elders to the Lord. Before they moved forward in service to the Lord, they fasted and prayed to seek God's approval of their service. In spite of the office to which one is being set for ordination, fasting and prayer must be the prerequisite for commendation to the Lord. Even the elders, though they are not considered greater ministries than apostles, still require being set apart for the expression of God's love, for they were ordained to express and teach of God's love. Fasting is where they demonstrate the willingness to die to themselves and express this great love to everyone they encounter.

This, then, is a call to overseers, bishops, and even pastors that they should fast and pray to seek God's commendation on the selection of bishops and pastors in the church. As mentioned, the elders in this case referred to pastors who were set over church congregations. But this concept also flowed down to pastors over congregations setting elders in the congregation, who would be set over various offices in the church. Either way, those who appoint must fast and pray to seek commendation from the Lord. We know that when God is for us, no one can be against us. But if God is not for us, then we are on our own.

Many leaders have been appointed without the time taken by the ones who appointed them to fast and pray to seek an answer from God as a confirmation of the call. They are in danger of having received their appointment by men. Because this wisdom has been neglected among many organizations of the church, many who are responsible to appoint depend on impressive résumés and attractive talents, rather on the Lord's commendation. Sadly, Satan has found avenues to introduce his agenda through some who were not chosen by God, though they were called. But I believe that the Lord is restoring these things that were once introduced and used. I believe that leaders are going to be appointed by the Word of God that came not only through prayer but through fasting.

This book is meant to help plant the seed of these revelations into your heart, that you may seek the scriptures to see what God requires concerning a fasting lifestyle. We should not take this for granted simply because it was not done with us or because we have not seen it done in our lifetimes. Neglecting to do what God prescribes, no matter how little, will have consequences. Certain stubborn spirits that we encounter will refuse to leave unless fasting is added to our prayer.

Printed in the United States
By Bookmasters